DR. BISHNU NARAINE
Department
St. Cloud St
720 Fourth
St. Cloud MN 56301-4498
O9-BHL-837

Behavioral Objectives and Instruction

Behavioral Objectives and Instruction

ROBERT J. KIBLER, Professor
Florida State University

LARRY L. BARKER, Associate Professor
Florida State University

DAVID T. MILES, Assistant Professor
Southern Illinois University

Allyn and Bacon, Inc., Boston

©Copyright 1970 by Allyn and Bacon, Inc., 470 Atlantic Avenue, Boston. All rights reserved. No part of this book may be reproduced in any form, or by any means, without permission in writing from the publisher.

Library of Congress Catalog Card Number: 76-91638

Printed in the United States of America

To Ralph Tyler

Robert Mager

James Popham

Bob
Jeanne
Jennifer
Lora
Sharon

Shirley
Ted
Valerie
Vance

Contents

PREFACE xi

CHAPTER I: BEHAVIORAL OBJECTIVES AND THE INSTRUCTIONAL PROCESS 1

Instructional Objectives for the General Model of Instruction 2
The General Model of Instruction 2
Different Types of Educational Objectives 20
Controversial Issues Regarding Behavioral Objectives 23

CHAPTER II: AN ANALYSIS OF PLANNING OBJECTIVES 28

Differences Between Planning and Informational Objectives 28
Reasons for Specifying Planning Objectives 30
An Analysis of Behavior for Specifying Planning Objectives 31
Difficulties Encountered in Specifying Planning Objectives 41

CHAPTER III: OBJECTIVES AND THE BEHAVIORAL DOMAINS 44

Interrelationships Among the Three Behavioral Domains 46
Cognitive Domain 47
Affective Domain 55
Psychomotor Domain 66
Summary 75

CHAPTER IV: WRITING INFORMATIONAL OBJECTIVES 77

Programed Practice in Identifying and Writing Informational Objectives 79
Writing Informational Objectives for the Cognitive Domain 92
Writing Informative Objectives for the Affective Domain 98
Writing Informational Objectives for the Psychomotor Domain 101

CHAPTER V: THE INFLUENCE OF BEHAVIORAL OBJECTIVES IN EDUCATION 102

Applications of Behavioral Objectives to Specified Educational Levels 102
The Relationship of Behavioral Objectives to Participants in the Educational Process 105
The Environment of the School and the Use of Behavioral Objectives 109

BIBLIOGRAPHY 111

POSTSCRIPT: PROBING THE VALIDITY OF ARGUMENTS AGAINST BEHAVIORAL GOALS 115

APPENDIX A: SAMPLES OF BEHAVIORAL OBJECTIVES 125

APPENDIX B: A SYSTEM FOR DEFINING ACHIEVEMENT DESCRIPTIONS FOR A TEACHER EDUCATION PROGRAM 156

APPENDIX C: INSTRUMENTATION OF BLOOM'S AND KRATHWOHL'S TAXONOMIES FOR THE WRITING OF EDUCATIONAL OBJECTIVES 177

APPENDIX D: INSTRUCTIONAL OBJECTIVES EXCHANGE 189

INDEX 191

Preface

This book is intended as a supplementary text for most courses in education (for example, educational methods, educational psychology, psychology of learning, educational administration, philosophy of education, programed instruction, computer-based instruction, and methods of evaluation). Teachers, administrators, curriculum planners, members of school boards and researchers also should find it of value.

Educational objectives have been studied throughout the history of American education. The work in programed learning and instructional technology in recent years has heightened interest in the specification of precise objectives. Efforts by Tyler (1934), Bloom *et al.* (1956), Mager (1962 and 1968), Mager and Beach (1967), Krathwohl *et al.* (1964), Gagné (1965a, 1965b, and 1965c), Glaser (1962 and 1965), Popham (1969) and Popham and Baker (1969) have been most influential in this trend.

This book represents an effort to identify the important functions behavioral objectives can serve in improving instruction. We hope the book will make a modest contribution to the continuing effort to improve the quality and efficiency of instruction by shaping favorable attitudes toward the use of behavioral objectives, by informing individuals about the nature and characteristics of behavioral objectives, and by teaching educators to write behavioral objectives.

This book makes six unique contributions:

1. It presents material relative to behavioral objectives from a variety of sources in a single volume.
2. It presents a classroom-tested model of instruction that illustrates the relationships of behavioral objectives to the instruction-learning process.
3. It prescribes an approach to objectives based on planning instruction and informing others of instructional goals.
4. It analyzes, in substantially more detail than has been available to date, the elements contained in objectives that are required to plan instruction.
5. It presents an original, taxonomic classification for the psychomotor domain.
6. Appendix A provides a variety of sample behavioral objectives for different areas of study. Teachers can use these as models in preparing their own behavioral objectives.

The authors express their appreciation to several persons who contributed to this text: first, to Professor W. James Popham for permitting us to reprint his paper, "Probing the Validity of Arguments Against Behavioral Goals"; second, to Mrs. Barbara Anderson for her assistance in typing and preparing early drafts of the manuscript; third, to Esther and Donald J. Cegala for their special contributions to the book in the final stages of editing; fourth, to the editorial staff of Allyn and Bacon for encouraging us to undertake the preparation of the text; and finally, to our wives for their patience, understanding, and countless services performed beyond the call of duty during the preparation of the manuscript.

R. J. K.
L. L. B.
D. T. M.

CHAPTER I

Behavioral Objectives and the Instructional Process

Behavioral objectives are statements which describe what students will be able to do after completing a prescribed unit of instruction. For example, a behavioral objective for a unit in history might be: "The student will be able to list three major factors which gave rise to the Industrial Revolution." (See Appendix A for additional examples.)

Behavioral objectives serve two major functions. First, they are used by instructors to design and evaluate their instruction. Second, they are used to communicate the goals of instructional units to such interested persons as (1) students planning to complete the unit; (2) instructors who teach preceding and following units; and (3) persons responsible for planning and evaluating curricula. Each of these functions requires a different type of behavioral objective.

The function of behavioral objectives as a prerequisite for planning and evaluating instruction can best be shown by presenting a breakdown of the major steps involved in planning and carrying out instruction. On the following pages a "General Model of Instruction" is presented.

You may attempt to achieve some specific instructional objectives for the model or just read through it to see what it says. If you choose the first option, you should (1) read the objectives for the model; (2) read the material and complete the practice exercises on the pages to follow; (3) engage in further practice to the extent necessary to be able to demonstrate mastery of the objectives; and (4) complete the test at the end. If you choose the other option, you can ignore the practice exercises and test.

INSTRUCTIONAL OBJECTIVES FOR THE GENERAL MODEL OF INSTRUCTION

Upon completing this unit you should be able to:

1. Draw a diagram of the General Model of Instruction (GMI).
2. Briefly describe the premise underlying the GMI and its two major functions.
3. List the major factors to consider in each component of the GMI.

THE GENERAL MODEL OF INSTRUCTION

The General Model of Instruction (GMI) is a procedural guide for designing and conducting instruction. The model is applicable to all levels of education (*e.g.,* elementary, secondary, higher), all subject matters (*e.g.,*English, science, art, vocational), and any length of instructional unit (*e.g.,* one hour, one week, one semester).

The major philosophical *premise* underlying the model is that *the goal of instruction is to maximize the efficiency with which all students achieve specified objectives.* The model is based on a technology of instruction which has developed in the past several years from the research and development work in three areas – experimental psychology, military training, and programed instruction. The three individuals who have contributed most to the specific model presented in this document are Robert Gagné (1965a, 1965b and 1965c), Robert Glaser (1965) and James Popham (1965).

The two major *functions* of the model are (1) to *guide instructional designers and teachers* through the major steps in designing and carrying out instruction; and (2) to *provide* an overall *structure* with which to view and study the instructional process. Although the model itself has not been validated experimentally for instructional efficiency, several of the prescriptive principles contained in it are derived from empirical research.

A flow diagram of the model is shown below. Each step in the model actually composes a body of knowledge with which anyone concerned with instruction should be intimately familiar.

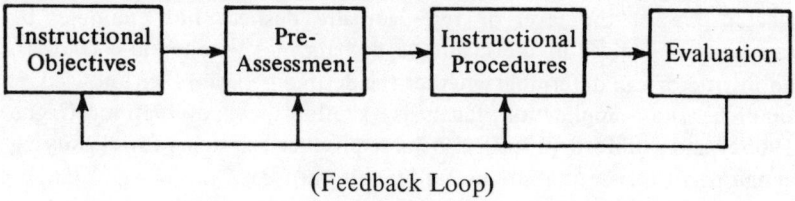

Figure 1. A General Model of Instruction

On the following pages each step is explained briefly and several of the major factors to consider in completing each step are presented. The material is designed to provide an overview of the instructional process and to expose the important relationship between the "objectives" component of the model and the other three components.

INSTRUCTIONAL OBJECTIVES

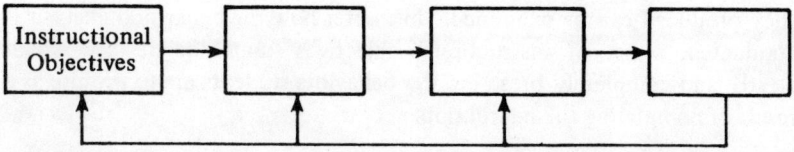

Preparing instructional objectives is probably the most important step in the entire model, for the instructor must decide what he wants to teach. The four major factors involved in preparing objectives – selection, classification, analysis, and specification – are discussed briefly below.

Selection. The selection of appropriate objectives usually is based on the following factors: (1) what the students are able to do before beginning the unit; (2) what the students should be able to do in instructional units that follow the unit of concern, and what they should be able to do after completing their education; and (3) the available instructional resources, including the instructor's capabilities with his subject matter.

Classification. The taxonomies, by Bloom and others (1956) and Krathwohl and others (1964), are useful in making sure that the objectives selected are of the level or type actually desired. For example, by classifying objectives in the cognitive domain into taxonomic categories, the instructor can determine whether the desired behaviors are knowledge, comprehension, application, analysis, synthesis, or evaluation. Gagné (1965c) and Guilford (1967) also have produced systems for classifying human performance that are useful for this purpose.

Analysis. Once a set of objectives has been selected, the instructor should perform a behavioral analysis in which he determines what a student will be expected to *do* to demonstrate achievement of the objective. The actual components to be examined in a behavioral analysis are (1) the important stimuli to which a student responds; (2) the important responses made; and (3) the criteria which the responses must meet to be considered successful.

Such an analysis can be performed by observing students who have already achieved the objective as they exhibit the desired behavior. Previous students can be interviewed, and the products (tests, papers, etc.) they produced can be examined. No matter how the behavioral analysis is conducted, a list of instructional objectives should be defined which clearly and completely prescribe the behaviors students are to acquire as a result of completing the instruction.

Specification. Behavioral objectives will be most valuable if they contain the following three elements recommended by Robert Mager in *Preparing Instructional Objectives* (1962).

1. A description of the type of *observable behavior* which the student will be asked to employ in demonstrating mastery of the objective (*e.g.,* "to write," "to solve," "to identify," "to orally describe"). Terms such as "to know," "to understand," and "to appreciate" must be avoided since they do not refer to observable behavior.
2. A description of the important *conditions* under which the student will be expected to demonstrate achievement of the objective (*e.g.,* time limits, materials or equipment that will be available, or special instructions).
3. The *criterion* which will be used to evaluate the success of the student's performance (*e.g.,* must get 70 percent correct, correctly

apply three principles, complete the task in 15 minutes, or correctly identify eight out of ten).

Prior to moving on, it should be emphasized that the function of these behavioral objectives is for *planning* instruction, not for *informing* others of instructional intentions. These objectives are more detailed than the behavioral objectives used typically for the purpose of communicating goals to others. Several types of extremely important objectives are difficult to measure and, thus, difficult to specify in behavioral terms. As a matter of fact, it seems that the more significant an objective is, the more difficult it is to measure. Examples of objectives which fall into the difficult-to-specify-and-measure category are those in the areas of problem solving, creativity, attitudes and values. The only solution we see to this problem is for such objectives to be specified as clearly as possible and for the instructor to be as resourceful as he can in developing evaluative measures, including attitude inventories and creativity tests.

Such objectives (*e.g.*, "to shape favorable attitudes toward your subject matter and toward learning") should *not* be eliminated because they are difficult to measure; they should be included and the instructor should work toward improving his measures.

PRACTICE EXERCISES

At this stage it may be a good idea to be sure you are learning what is intended in this unit. By now, you should be able to fill in the first component in the model. If you also can complete the others, do it.

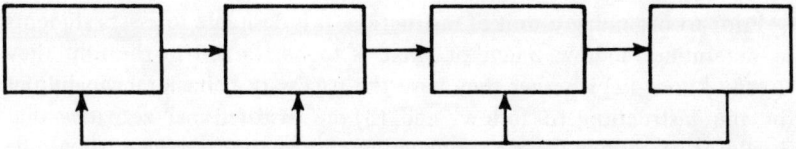

In addition, identify the premise underlying the model and the two major functions of the model. If you cannot remember the premise or the functions, take a quick look back on page 2 and then write them below.

Premise: _____

_____

Functions: 1. _____

_____

2. _____

_____

Now, list the four factors or substeps in the first component of the model. Peek if you must.

1. _____

2. _____

3. _____

4. _____

You should check on the accuracy of your responses by referring back to the preceding pages before proceeding.

PRE-ASSESSMENT

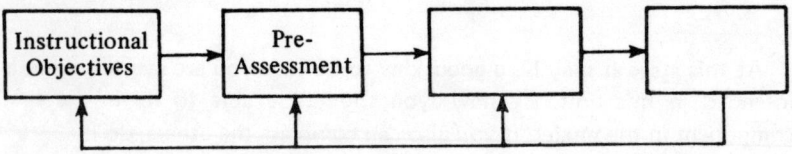

Prior to beginning a unit of instruction, it is desirable to assess students to determine (1) how much of what is to be learned in the unit they already know; (2) whether they have the necessary behavioral capabilities for the instruction to follow; and (3) the instructional activities that should be prescribed for each student. Of course, the assessment should be based on the specific instructional objectives specified for the unit. The results of this assessment should indicate (1) whether any students may *omit* any of the objectives in the unit; (2) whether any students should be required to master *prerequisite* skills before beginning the unit; and (3) what specific *instructional activities* should be provided for specific students. The above alternative courses of action imply that individualized instruction or tracking procedures are available for the instructional event. However, it is frequently possible to require prerequisite behaviorial competencies and omit objectives for individual students in group-paced instruction.

You will be asked to recall the three courses of action which can be taken as a result of pre-assessment (1. omit objectives; 2. require prerequisites; 3. prescribe instruction) upon completing this unit so you may wish to rehearse them a few times before proceeding.

INSTRUCTIONAL PROCEDURES

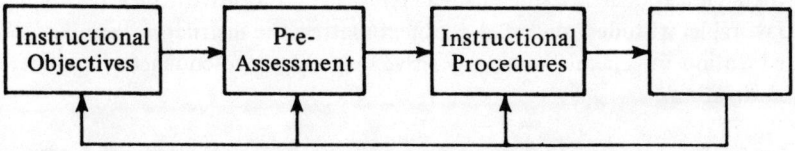

After students are pre-assessed and adjustments are made, such as adding or eliminating objectives or requiring prerequisite learning, the instructional procedures are implemented. The design of the instructional procedures involves (1) selection of available instructional materials (*e.g.*, books, films, or lesson plan); (2) preparing new instructional materials when necessary; and (3) developing a sequential plan which appears to be the most efficient for achieving the stated objectives. Decisions should be based upon research evidence when it is available.

The ten generalizations specified below are, to a large extent, based upon research evidence and are examples of principles which should be consulted in designing instructional activities. It should be noted that every application of these principles will not apply automatically to all students and all subject matters. Students vary in the way they learn, subject matters vary in their structures, and teachers vary in the way they interpret and apply principles of instruction. Thus, applications of these principles in each situation and with each student must be tested continually.

1. Pre-Learning Preparation. Learners must master the prerequisite behaviors to succeed in new learning experiences. Instructors should prepare students for new learning experiences by warming them up, telling them what previously learned behaviors will be helpful or harmful, and helping them to acquire an appropriate "set" (predisposition to respond in a particular way) for what is to follow. For example, a preview at the beginning of a chapter or film can increase learning efficiency. Providing students with the behavioral objectives for a unit has also been found to facilitate learning.

2. Motivation. Students are more efficient if they want to learn what is being taught. This desire can be promoted by convincing learners of the value of mastering the subject matter and by offering rewards (*e.g.*, social approval or grades) for accomplishing learning objectives. Selecting subject matter that interests students and permits them to participate in planning their educational activities can increase their incentive to learn. Shaping favorable attitudes toward the subject matter, the instructor, learning, and education in general can have positive long-range consequences for student motivation.

3. Providing a Model of Terminal Performance (Mastery). When possible, learners should be shown examples of what they are to produce or to do at the end of a learning experience. Imitative learning is one of the most effective procedures by which humans acquire new behaviors. Showing students sample term papers, completed projects, or final exam papers or demonstrating a desired performance can facilitate learning dramatically.

4. Active Responding. At the outset of training, learners can profit from watching or listening to someone else perform the acts to be learned, but most learners will become proficient only if they perform the acts themselves. Thus, it is what the learner does – not what the teacher does – that determines learning. In learning verbal material from a textbook, most students can profit by overtly reviewing what they have read while not looking at the material.

5. Guidance. When attempting to demonstrate new behaviors to be learned, instructors should guide and prompt the students. For example, they could give verbal guidance for each step in carrying out long division problems. Such prompts should be eliminated gradually until the learner is able to perform the task without them.

6. *Practice.* Opportunities should be provided for learners to use newly learned behaviors repeatedly. Practice will be effective to the extent that the behaviors practiced are similar to behaviors to be performed in the future (the terminal objectives). For example, after learning initially to subtract, students should practice with a variety of number combinations.

7. *Knowledge of Results.* A learner should have prompt and frequent knowledge of the success of his responses. He must find his success rewarding in order for the behavior to be reinforced. Ideally, he should know an instant after he makes a response whether it is appropriate or not. When he is personally confident of the correctness of his response, external confirmation may be unnecessary, but when he is unsure, such feedback is generally desirable.

8. *Graduated Sequence.* Subject matter should be organized in a hierarchical form from the simple to the complex – from the familiar to the unfamiliar. The steps should be paced so that the learner succeeds in each step but does not become bored. It has been found that permitting students to follow their own sequence in achieving well-defined objectives yields better results than insisting upon teacher-designed learning sequences (Mager and McCann, 1961).

9. *Individual Differences.* People learn at different speeds; therefore, learning experiences should be designed so that each student may proceed at his own pace. Some students will require considerable practice to master a concept while others may acquire the same concept upon first encounter.

10. *Classroom Teaching Performance.* Skills in stimulating interest, explaining, guiding, identifying and administering reinforcers, and managing classroom behavior can make an enormous difference in instructional effectiveness. Unfortunately, such social skills are often the most difficult to learn, but some current work on the analysis of social and personality factors in teaching shows promise of reducing the difficulty. The changing

role of the teacher from information-dispenser to manager of instructional experiences is also an encouraging development.

PRACTICE EXERCISES

Although it would be desirable for you to learn all of the information within the ten factors, for the present goal (obtaining an overview of the model) you are only asked to be able to list the ten topic headings. The ten topics are:

1. *Pre-Learning Preparation*
2. *Motivation*
3. *Providing a Model of Terminal Performance*
4. *Active Responding*
5. *Guidance*
6. *Practice*
7. *Knowledge of Results*
8. *Graduated Sequence*
9. *Individual Differences*
10. *Classroom Teaching Performance*

One way to memorize this list is to view the first seven items as a chronological sequence of events which should happen in a learning sequence. The other three are more general and apply to the entire instructional process.

After reading the list a couple of times, turn to the next page and try to write all the factors down.

1. _____
2. _____
3. _____
4. _____
5. _____
6. _____
7. _____
8. _____
9. _____
10. _____

When you've written all you can, turn back and check yourself. Write down any factors you couldn't think of.

Now, try it once more by covering the list with your hand.

1. _____
2. _____
3. _____
4. _____
5. _____
6. _____
7. _____
8. _____
9. _____
10. _____

There, now you probably got them all, didn't you? So let's go to the last component of the model.

EVALUATION

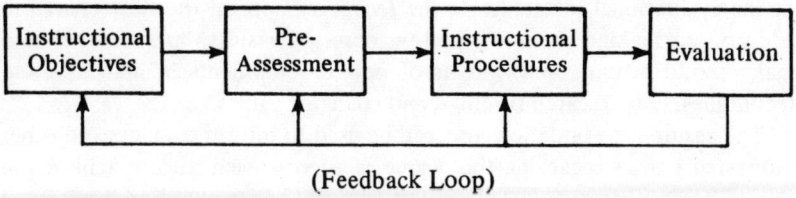

When students complete an instructional unit, they are evaluated to determine whether the instruction was successful in achieving the unit's objectives. Typically, evaluation involves using tests and instruments to measure the acquisition of knowledge, skills, and attitudes. Frequently, it is necessary to specify or describe student achievement. This is usually a difficult task. An example of an actual system employed to specify achievement descriptions for a teacher education program is included in Appendix B. This example should give you some idea of the complexity of defining achievement.

If the objectives have been specified clearly, test preparation is quite simple. An important consideration in designing evaluative measures is that the instrument measure the identical behavior specified in the objectives. It also is important to note that the success of the instruction is being evaluated, not the success of the pupils.

In most instances in formal education, it is both desirable and feasible for all students to master all objectives. If all students do not perform acceptably on all objectives, an explanation must be sought from among the following three reasons:

1. The unsuccessful students were prepared inadequately for the unit, which could mean that the objectives were unrealistic or that the students should not have begun the unit without prior training.
2. The unsuccessful students were not motivated properly to master the material.
3. The instruction was not designed properly or insufficient time was provided for the students to master the objectives.

Changes in the objectives, the pre-instruction evaluation procedures, the instruction, or the post-instruction evaluation are to be made on the basis of the evaluational results (note the *feedback loop* on the flow chart). In addition to making changes based on observed results, instructors should make modifications on the basis of new developments in materials and techniques, new research findings, and changing values.

The results of evaluation also can be used to inform students and other interested parties regarding the degree of success each student achieved in the unit. However, since all students may be required to master all objectives, this information may consist of only an indication of the different lengths of time each student took to complete the unit.

The most important factors you should remember about evaluation are:

1. It is the success of the *instruction* which is being evaluated.
2. Unsuccessful instruction is probably a result of one of the following:
   a. students did not have the *prerequisites* necessary to begin the unit.
   b. the students were *motivated inadequately* before or during the unit.
   c. The *instructional* activities were designed *inadequately*.
3. Changes in objectives, pre-assessment, and instructional procedures should be made, if necessary, so that all students achieve all required objectives.

On the next page you are asked to reproduce a rough approximation of the three important factors to remember about evaluation, so you may want to look them over again.

PRACTICE EXERCISES

Jot down the three factors considered most essential in the Evaluation component of the model:

1. _____
2. _____
   a. _____
   b. _____
   c. _____
3. _____

Check yourself and if you didn't do well, try it again before proceeding.

1. _____
2. _____
   a. _____
   b. _____
   c. _____
3. _____

SUMMARY

Below is a summary of the material you are asked to reproduce on the following pages. You may wish to review and practice reproducing it before proceeding.

General Model of Instruction

Premise: The goal of instruction is to maximize the efficiency with which all students achieve specified objectives.

Functions: 1. To guide instruction design and implementation.
2. To provide structure for viewing and studying instruction.

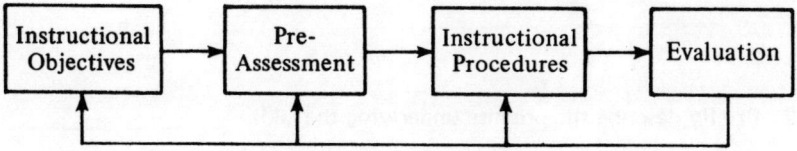

(Feedback Loop)

1. Select
2. Classify
3. Analyze
4. Specify

1. Omit objectives
2. Require prerequisites
3. Prescribe instruction

1. Preparation
2. Motivation
3. Model of mastery
4. Active responding
5. Guidance
6. Practice
7. Knowledge of results
8. Graduated sequence
9. Individual differences
10. Teaching performance

1. Evaluate instruction
2. Causes of failure:
   a. Prerequisite
   b. Motivation
   c. Instruction
3. Modify to achieve 100% mastery

TEST
GENERAL MODEL OF INSTRUCTION
Evaluation for Cognitive Objectives

1. Draw a diagram of the General Model of Instruction, including the names of each component.

2. Briefly describe the premise underlying the GMI. _____

   _____

   _____

3. Briefly describe the two major functions of the GMI.

   a. _____

   _____

   b. _____

   _____

4. List the major factors to consider in each of the components of the GMI.

   Instructional Objectives:

   1. _____
   2. _____
   3. _____
   4. _____

Pre-Assessment:

1. _____

2. _____

3. _____

Instructional Procedures:

1. _____

2. _____

3. _____

4. _____

5. _____

6. _____

7. _____

8. _____

9. _____

10. _____

Evaluation:

1. _____

2. _____

   a. _____

   b. _____

   c. _____

3. _____

If you were able to answer all of the preceding questions, you have achieved the objectives specified for the General Model of Instruction.

If you would like to broaden your knowledge of the philosophy and procedures associated with the General Model of Instruction, the following references are recommended: DeCecco (1968), Glaser (1965), and Popham (1965).

DIFFERENT TYPES OF EDUCATIONAL OBJECTIVES

Instructional objectives are written at various levels of specificity. We already have introduced two of the most important types of objectives for instruction: *planning* and *informational* objectives. Most readers will have been exposed to a third, more general, type of objective: *general educational objectives.* A discussion of general educational objectives is included in *The Cardinal Principles of Secondary Education* (1937) and, more recently, in *The Central Purposes of American Education* (1961), published by the Educational Policies Commission of the National Education Association.

Figure 2 shows how the three types of objectives differ with respect to specificity.

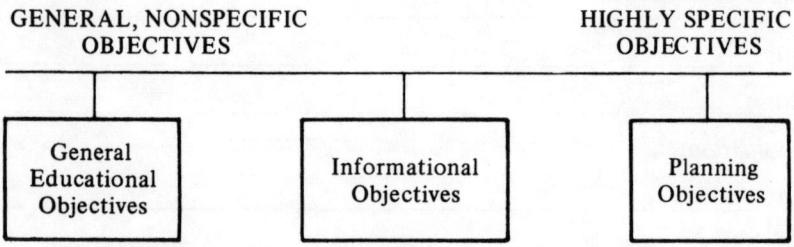

FIGURE 2. SPECIFICITY CONTINUUM OF OBJECTIVES

At the extreme end of nonspecificity are the very general objectives of educational institutions and broad educational programs (for example, "to make better citizens," "to advance humanity," and "to promote our cultural ideals"). At the other end of the continuum are the highly specific objectives recommended by Mager (1962), which are invaluable for designing instruction. Somewhere in the middle are the objectives written for a curriculum, a course, a weekly unit, or a daily lesson plan.

Some educational objectives do not fit neatly into any of the three categories described above. For example, outlines of objectives for elementary (Kearney, 1953) and secondary (French, 1957) educational levels have been published. These objectives would be placed between general educational objectives and informational objectives. A recently developed set of objectives for the language arts would be placed in a similar position (Lazarus and Knudson, 1967). The types of objectives included in the two volumes of the *Taxonomy of Educational Objectives* (Bloom, *et al.,* 1956, and Krathwohl, *et al.,* 1964) would probably be placed slightly to the left of informational objectives. A more extensive examination of the implications of different kinds of objectives is discussed by Lindvall (1964). In addition, Appendix A contains a variety of examples of objectives, ranging from rather general to a more specific level.

Planning objectives are critical to the entire instructional process. More information on the specification of this type of behavioral objective will be provided in Chapter II.

Informational objectives are used by instructional designers to communicate their intentions to others. These behavioral objectives, important in education, are abbreviations of the planning objectives. They are typically written after the planning objectives have been specified. Note the relationship between the following planning objective and informational objective.

Planning Objective:
In a half-hour test at the end of the week, the student will be able to list the steps a bill follows through Congress, specifying the requirements for passage at each step. All steps must be included in the correct order, and the passage requirements must match the ones in the textbook.
Informational Objective:
The student will be able to list, in correct order, the steps a bill follows through Congress, specifying the requirements for passage in each step.

The informational objective omits the conditions under which the behavior was to be performed ("in a half-hour test at the end of the week") and the criteria to be used in judging acceptable performance ("all steps must be in the correct order, and the passage requirements must match the ones in the textbook"). It contains a reference to the type of behavior expected of the student ("to list") and a description of the product he is to produce ("a listing of the steps a bill follows. . ."). This example should provide a rough idea of the distinction between planning objectives and informational objectives.

Informational objectives will be explained further in Chapter IV.

THE VALUE OF PLANNING OBJECTIVES

Teachers or instructional designers benefit in three ways from defining planning objectives.

1. Given clearly defined goals to work toward, teachers can design instructional experiences to achieve them and can evaluate the effectiveness of such experiences according to whether the goals are achieved.
2. Students can be examined prior to beginning instruction to determine whether they have already mastered any of the objectives. Information regarding their preparedness for the instruction to follow can also be obtained.
3. Each student can be evaluated on mastery of the unit's objectives. In this way every student can be required to master all objectives. This is in contrast to grading students on how well they performed in comparison with the rest of the class (grading on the curve) or in achievement of a certain percentage of the objectives of the unit.

THE VALUE OF INFORMATIONAL OBJECTIVES

Students, curriculum planners, student advisors, teachers and administrators benefit from the use of informational objectives.

11. Several studies have demonstrated that students can be more efficient learners if they are provided with objectives (Mager and McCann, 1961; McNeil, 1966; Miles, Kibler, and Pettigrew, 1967). Perhaps one of the reasons students do better when given copies of the objectives of a unit of instruction is that they are spared the frustration and time-consuming effort of trying to guess what the teacher expects of them.

2. Given such clearly specified objectives, curriculum planners are better able to arrange sequences of courses or units of instruction. Knowing what students (hopefully all students) are able to do at the end of courses and what students are able to do at the beginning of courses (prerequisites), it should be possible to eliminate unnecessary overlap of courses and to identify and fill in gaps between courses.
3. Students and their advisors are able to plan their course programs better when they can read course descriptions which include informational objectives.
4. Through clear behavioral objectives, teachers are able to tell other teachers what they teach. Stating that "students learn to name each state and its capital in the United States" tells considerably more than stating "United States geography is taught."
5. Teachers and administrators can determine the level of objectives students will be able to achieve in terms of the three taxonomic classifications to be discussed in Chapter III. For example, in the cognitive domain, objectives can be classified as knowledge, comprehension, application, analysis, synthesis, and evaluation, thereby avoiding undue emphasis on a certain level of objectives.

CONTROVERSIAL ISSUES REGARDING BEHAVIORAL OBJECTIVES

Even though the authors take the position that behavioral objectives are an extremely important part of the educational process, it must be clear that all educators do not share this point of view. Some heated discussions have taken place among educators regarding whether or not behavioral objectives are either important or useful. Therefore, there is merit in examining some of the controversial issues associated with such objectives. Following are the three most commonly asked questions concerning behavioral objectives.

1. Can all important outcomes of education be defined and measured behaviorally?
2. Can prespecification of objectives prevent teachers from achieving objectives which might arise unexpectedly during a course of instruction?

3. Will more trivial learner behaviors, which are the easiest to operationalize, receive a greater emphasis than more important educational outcomes?

James Popham has written an insightful paper, contained in the Postscript of this book, which deals with these and several other arguments that have been presented in opposition to behavioral objectives.

Three issues with which Dr. Popham does not deal are given brief consideration here.

1. PRE-SPECIFYING THE OBJECTIVES FOR A UNIT OF INSTRUCTION WHICH A TEACHER HAS NOT PREVIOUSLY TAUGHT

This is indeed a complex task. But it has been our experience that a procedure such as the following can reduce some of the complexity and result in a fairly complete set of objectives for the succeeding times the course is taught.

A. Specify a set of objectives, stating them in general terms. These objectives should be based on an analysis of post-instructional performance expectancies and pre-instructional performance capability.
B. Specify more precise objectives for each unit as it occurs.
C. Evaluate the results of each unit and base the objectives for the following units on these results.
D. Identify and record objectives which are achieved in addition to those prespecified for each unit.

This procedure is essentially a crude technique for testing hypotheses regarding objectives, identifying unpredicted objectives, and determining criteria for appropriate levels of performance. Thus, experience with the first attempt at a course is used to develop a set of precise objectives for succeeding presentations of the course.

2. DECIDING WHETHER ALL STUDENTS SHOULD BE REQUIRED TO ACHIEVE THE SAME OBJECTIVES

With the increasing emphasis on individualized instruction, this decision is indeed relevant. Our viewpoint is that for most courses in public school, industrial, and undergraduate education, all students should achieve a common set of goals. This does not, however, preclude the possibility of specification of behavioral objectives for *individual* student achievement. Opportunities should be available for students in many of these courses to go beyond the basic requirements to pursue individual areas of interest. One technique which has been employed frequently involves each student's stating his specific objectives. Such a procedure seems quite appropriate when one of the teacher's objectives is for students to be able to identify and acquire behavioral competencies of personal concern.

3. DECIDING WHETHER ALL STUDENTS SHOULD BE REQUIRED TO ACHIEVE THE SAME LEVEL OF MASTERY FOR EACH OBJECTIVE

This issue is related to the previous one. Brought into question here is the value of using the norm-referenced evaluation and grading system, in which students are assessed on the basis of their performance relative to the group, instead of the criterion-referenced system, in which students are evaluated according to their achievement of specified criteria – irrespective of how the group performs. The norm-referenced system is presently the most widely-used system, although the criterion-referenced system is growing in popularity.

Without clearly defined objectives and performance criteria for measuring attainment of the objectives, the norm-referenced system is probably the most reasonable method available for assessing student achievement. However, given specific objectives and evaluation criteria, the practice of measuring the relative achievement of the objective may be open to question. Much has been written on this issue recently, and very likely the increased use of behavioral objectives is to a great extent responsible for the dialogue.

Some educators feel that the purpose of education is not to determine who learns more and less of a given subject matter, but rather to see to it that all students learn what is considered necessary. From this viewpoint, the criterion-referenced system would be the desirable choice, and all students could be required to achieve the same level of mastery on each objective. This approach does not negate the possibility of providing the opportunity for students to go beyond the basic required objectives. The latter possibility may be extremely important to a more widespread acceptance of criterion-referenced evaluation, since the relative achievement information (presently provided by norm-referenced evaluation and grading) is employed for a large variety of seemingly vital functions. School grades are used as a basis for selecting students for college, major areas of study, graduate school, honors programs, scholarships, and post-school employment; for retaining students in school; for influencing students' occupational choices; and for recording progress toward certificates and degrees. They also are used as incentives and rewards. Thus, it appears that some kind of information regarding a student's academic performance relative to other students is needed. Possibly standardized academic ability or achievement tests eventually can provide such information and the results of instructional evaluation could be used only for determining the effectiveness of instruction when students have achieved specified objectives.

Two generalizations regarding this issue seem appropriate. When mastery of an objective is vital to the achievement of subsequent objectives (for example, some language and computational skills are essential to much of what follows in and comes after school), then all students should be required to fully master the objective. When subsequent performance demands are not so clear-cut, it may be appropriate to permit students to achieve varying levels of mastery of an objective – above some minimum criterion.

The other generalization involves the domain of evaluation in education. The three primary functions of evaluation in instruction are to provide information regarding (1) student achievement of instructional objectives; (2) the success of instruction in getting students to achieve objectives; and (3) student achievement and ability which can be used for academic and occupational selection. Although both the norm-referenced and criterion-referenced systems can provide information for the three functions, the criterion-referenced system probably is a more desirable procedure for accomplishing the first and second functions, and the norm-referenced system is more appropriate for meeting the third function. The different amounts of time students spend in reaching criteria could provide information for Function 3 within a criterion-referenced system, but such a practice may tend to result in an over-emphasis on speed of acquisition and an under-emphasis on retention and transfer.

Thus, it is our position that a criterion-referenced system should be employed for the basic fundamentals of instruction, and all students should be required to meet the standards considered necessary for post-instruction performance. In addition, opportunities for students to go beyond the required standards should be provided, and the results of students' performance in these areas, plus the results of standardized achievement and ability tests, should be used to satisfy the functions for which grades are used presently.

CHAPTER II

An Analysis of Planning Objectives

In Chapter I the importance of defining and specifying behavioral objectives was pointed out. This chapter further amplifies some of the implications regarding behavioral objectives, in general, and planning objectives, in particular. There are four parts to the chapter. The first part includes a more detailed examination of the differences between planning and informational objectives, the second part discusses the reasons for specifying planning objectives, and the third part discusses critical elements of a planning objective. Part four covers difficulties encountered in specifying planning objectives.

DIFFERENCES BETWEEN PLANNING AND INFORMATIONAL OBJECTIVES

Two types of behavioral objectives were defined in Chapter I, *planning* and *informational* objectives. Now, see if you can underline the part of the statement below that should be included in an informational objective.

> Given a twenty minute test following an assignment to read the section in the social studies textbook describing the location of the main islands of the Greater Antilles, the student will write the name

of the Greater Antilles island which is closest to Florida; the student's response must match the information specified in the textbook in order to be accurate.

Now turn the page and see if you underlined the correct part of the objective.

If you underlined "the student will write the name of the Greater Antilles island which is closest to Florida," you responded correctly. If not, you should reread the section in the first chapter dealing with the differences between *planning* objectives and *informational* objectives. The informational objective includes a description of a type of behavior the student is to perform, "to write," and a description of what he is to produce, "name of the Greater Antilles island closest to Florida." Informational objectives are designed to inform others (*e.g.*, teachers, students, and administrators) of instructional intent. They will be discussed in greater detail in Chapter 4.

Planning objectives are more precise and include more specific details than informational objectives. The *planning objective* on pages 28-29 describes the behavior the student will be asked to employ to demonstrate mastery of the objective, and the product of the student's behavior (the main components of an informational objective), plus the conditions under which the behavior is to be performed ("Given a twenty minute test following an assignment to read the section in the social studies textbook describing the location of the main islands of the Greater Antilles") and the criteria to be used in determining if the performance was satisfactory ("the student's response must match the information specified in the textbook in order to be accurate"). Typically, planning objectives should be written before informational objectives.

REASONS FOR SPECIFYING PLANNING OBJECTIVES

There are several reasons for specifying planning objectives. First, Gagné (1965a) has pointed out the necessity of evaluating student accomplishments in any educational program. It is important for the teacher to be able to determine the student's capabilities at any given time during an instructional program. When planning objectives are specified it is possible for the teacher to determine the student's present level of mastery for any prescribed objective at any time. Moreover, by specifying planning objectives teachers can identify a student who has acquired, prior to instruction, the level of excellence required for successful performance on a given objective. Planning objectives also may help in identifying students who lack the prerequisites to master the prescribed objectives successfully.

Second, because a planning objective includes a performance standard, it represents a minimal level of performance to be sought by all students. Therefore, each student in a given class can be expected to master successfully the behavior specified in an objective. This idea may seem startling to you – that every student in a class could be a success. However, such outstanding psychologists as Bloom (1968) and Carroll (1963) have argued that most students can achieve mastery if they will (and are permitted to) devote enough time to the learning task.

Third, as we indicated previously, planning objectives are used primarily by instructors as the basis for designing and evaluating their instruction. Working backwards from a given planning objective, an instructor can make a behavioral analysis, identifying all of the prerequisite behaviors required to perform the objective. The analysis is considered complete when the instructor identifies all the behaviors the students possess before beginning the unit. Further information regarding this approach to instructional design is contained in Ammerman and Melching (1966), De Cecco (1968), and Gagné (1965a, 1965b, and 1965c).

When teachers formulate planning objectives they make decisions about, and include in their objectives, minimal acceptable standards. Having established standards, it is reasonably easy for teachers to construct evaluative instruments which measure the behaviors specified in the objectives.

Performance standards also help teachers determine the adequacy of their instructional program. If students do not master objectives efficiently as a result of a given instructional program, various changes may be required in the program, in the objectives, or in other elements identified in the General Model of Instruction.

AN ANALYSIS OF BEHAVIOR FOR SPECIFYING PLANNING OBJECTIVES

This section contains a behavioral analysis of what a student is expected to be able to do when he has successfully completed a unit of instruction. Other authors have used terms like "task description" or "task analysis" to describe similar information (Tyler, Gagné, and Scriven, 1967; Lange, 1967; Stolurow, 1963; Miller, 1962a, 1962b; Taber, Glaser, and Schaefer,

1965; and Gagné, 1965a, 1965b, 1965c). By *behavioral analysis* we mean a study of the final behavior to be required of the student broken down into its component parts. Before examining each of the five parts of this final behavior, it may be valuable to review a few terms and concepts which will be used throughout this volume.

By *behavior* we mean actions and movements which people can be observed (seen, heard or felt) making. Thus, thinking, which involves electrochemical activity in the brain, is not considered behavior here, since the activity cannot be observed directly with the unaided senses. (However, such activity can be observed indirectly with mechanical devices such as an electroencephlograph.) Therefore, since behavioral objectives must identify the action a person must perform, all behavioral objectives require a psychomotor component.

Caution must be exercised, however, to avoid overemphasizing the "action" component of objectives; cognitive and affective objectives are concerned with characteristics of thinking and feeling which are themselves not directly observable. States of affection and acts of cognition are inferred from psychomotor acts. We do not see a person analyze a poem; we see or hear a report of his analysis. We do not see the mental activity of problem solving; we see tentative solutions to the problem. We do not see the emotional feeling a person experiences when listening to a favorite piece of music; we see the results of his emotional experience in his verbal response or facial expression or in his future selection of that music to listen to.

Actually, we are usually more interested in the characteristics of the products or actions which permit us to infer the type of mental activity that produced them, than we are in the form of behavior which made them observable. However, since the only way we can be sure of what happens "inside" people's heads or "hearts" is to look at what they do, we emphasize the observable actions. Objective evidence is required to determine whether a person has thought or felt in a particular way. If instructors were not concerned with making changes in students, they would not have to bother looking at behavior – but they do have that responsibility.

Performance is used in this book to refer to the result of a person's action which is evaluated to see whether he has successfully completed an objective. For example, if an objective is for a student to build an electric motor that runs, the "performance" that is evaluated is whether the electric motor runs. Or, if an objective is to write a term paper according to a set of prescribed specifications, the term paper that the student turns in is what is evaluated and thus is considered his performance. *Product* is frequently used as a synonym for *performance.*

You will see that these distinctions are necessary as we examine the components of planning objectives. Gagné, (1965a, 1965b and 1965c) has emphasized the importance of understanding the relationship between education and human performance. Human performance must be employed to determine what is *intended* to occur in education. It is also tied into an understanding of learning, since we infer that learning has taken place as a result of observing a change in performance. For example, suppose we observed two performance events separated by a few days. In the first event the student was presented with five sentences and was told to underline the "verb" in each of them; he subsequently failed to perform the task satisfactorily. During the second event a similar set of instructions and list of sentences were presented to the same student. This time the student performed the task successfully. A *change* in the student's performance was observed, which might give us some basis for inferring that the student learned to underline verbs.

Now that some of these basic terms have been reviewed, we will analyze the component parts of the final performance that the student is expected to demonstrate as a result of completing an instructional unit. Planning objectives should contain the following five elements:

1. *Who* is to perform the desired behavior (*e.g.*, "the student" or "the learner")
2. The *actual behavior* to be employed in demonstrating mastery of the objective (*e.g.*, "to write," or "to speak")
3. The *result* (*i.e.*, the product or performance) of the behavior, which will be evaluated to determine whether the objective is mastered (*e.g.*, "an essay," or "the speech")
4. The *relevant conditions* under which the behavior is to be performed (*e.g.*, 'in a one-hour quiz," or "in front of the class")
5. The *standard* which will be used to evaluate the success of the product or performance (*e.g.*, "90 percent correct," or "four out of five correct")

Each of these components is identified in the objective shown below. The number of each *component* is *identified above* the appropriate portion of the planning objective. Those words and phrases that are not a part of a specific component have no identification appearing above them.

4 1

| During the one hour mid-term examination, | | the student |

2 5 3

| will be able | | to spell correctly | | 45 out of 50 | | words |

4

| randomly selected from the 200 words listed in Units one and two

1 2 3

of the spelling book. | | The student | | will write | | the words | as

4 5

they are presented orally by the teacher. | | In order to be correct

the spelling of each word must match the spelling in the spelling

book. |

WHO IS TO PERFORM THE DESIRED BEHAVIOR

Determining the first component, the *who* is easy. Obviously, you usually want the *student* to demonstrate the behavior. Other terms for those who may be asked to perform the desired behavior are *learner, pupil,* and *enrollees.*

THE ACTUAL BEHAVIOR TO BE EMPLOYED

The second component of a planning objective is the specific observable act or behavior that the learner is to perform. For example, the student may be instructed "to write," "to identify," or "to distinguish." Researchers working in task analysis have reported a necessity for "hard," "clear," *action verbs* to classify the behavior to be performed (Chenzoff and Folley, Jr., 1965; Miller, 1962a and 1962b). Some of the action words used as operational guides are defined in the following list.

Definitions of Action Words*

1. *Identifying.* The individual selects (by pointing to, touching, or picking up) the correct object of a class name. For example: Upon being asked, "Which animal is the frog?" when presented with a set of small animals, the child is expected to respond by picking up or clearly pointing to or touching the frog; if the child is asked to "pick up the red triangle" when presented with a set of paper cutouts representing different shapes, he is expected to pick up the red triangle. This class of performances also includes identifying object properties (such as rough, smooth, straight, curved) and, in addition, kinds of changes such as an increase or decrease in size.
2. *Distinguishing.* Identifying objects or events which are potentially confusable (square, rectangle), or when two contrasting identifications (such as right, left) are involved.
3. *Constructing.* Generating a construction or drawing which identifies a designated object or set of conditions. Example: Beginning with a line segment, the request is made, "Complete this figure so that it represents a triangle."
4. *Naming.* Supplying the correct name (orally or in written form) for a class of objects or events. Example: "What is this three-dimensional object called?" Response: "A cone."
5. *Ordering.* Arranging two or more objects or events in proper order in accordance with a stated category. For example: "Arrange these moving objects in order of their speeds."
6. *Describing.* Generating and naming all of the necessary categories of objects, object properties, or event properties that are relevant to the description of a designated situation. Example: "Describe this object," and the observer does not limit the categories which may be generated by mentioning them, as in the question "Describe the color and shape of this object." The child's description is considered sufficiently complete when there

*Henry H. Walbesser, *Constructing Behavioral Objectives* (Mimeographed). College Park, Maryland: Bureau of Educational Research, University of Maryland, 1966. Reproduced by permission, for which the authors express their thanks.

is a probability that any other individual is able to use the description to identify the object or event.

7. *Stating a Rule.* Makes a verbal statement (not necessarily in technical terms) which conveys a rule or a principle, including the names of the proper classes of objects or events in their correct order. Example: "What is the test for determining whether this surface is flat?" The acceptable response requires the mention of the application of a straightedge, in various directions, to determine touching all along the edge for each position.
8. *Applying a Rule.* Using a learned principle or rule to derive an answer to a question. The answer may be correct identification, the supplying of a name, or some other kind of response. The question is stated in such a way that the individual must employ a rational process to arrive at the answer. Such a process may be simple, as "Property A is true, property B is true, therefore property C must be true."
9. *Demonstrating.* Performing the operations necessary to the application of a rule or principle. Example: "Show how you would tell whether this surface is flat." The answer requires that the individual use a straightedge to determine touching of the edge to the surface at all points, and in various directions.
10. *Interpreting.* The child should be able to identify objects and/or events in terms of their consequences. There will be a set of rules or principles always connected with this behavior.

THE RESULT OF THE BEHAVIOR

The third component is the product, the performance, or the "what" the student is to do. Here are some examples of statements which include the first three components. The portion of the statement which appears in italics is the *result* of the behavior.

The student writes *a sentence.*
The learner walks *from point A to point B.*
The student spells aloud *the word "simple."*

To determine the result you can expect from students in an educational setting, you must first decide what you *want* them to do as a result of instruction and then write planning objectives which identify *what* behavior is to be performed.

There are several ways to determine what to include in planning objectives. Some educators have found it useful to examine old tests, since they are one indication of what students can do after instruction. Others have interviewed students who have mastered the desired behavior, determining *what* their terminal behavior for a course was and *how* they performed it. Still others have observed a student actually demonstrating mastery performance or have observed a product he produced (and the steps executed in producing it).

THE RELEVANT CONDITIONS UNDER WHICH THE BEHAVIOR IS TO BE PERFORMED

What are the stimulus conditions to which the student will be expected to respond when demonstrating the desired behavior? To state this concern in less complex terms, "What are the *givens,* the *limitations,* the *restrictions* which are imposed on the student when he is demonstrating the terminal behavior?" Here are examples of some stimulus conditions that one might include in a planning objective.

"When presented with a typed list . . ."
"Given a slide rule . . ."
"Upon reading Chapter IV in *x* (insert name of textbook) . . ."
"With the use of class notes . . ."
"Without the use of class notes or other references . . ."

Now, let us turn to the question of how to determine the conditions under which the student will be expected to demonstrate mastery – conditions that are to be specified in the planning objectives. Three suggestions are listed below:

1. Specify the information, tools, equipment, source materials and anything else which will be available to the student to help him perform the terminal behavior required in the objective.

2. Specify the information, tools, equipment, source materials and anything else which the student cannot use when demonstrating the terminal behavior.
3. List as many of the actual conditions as possible under which the student might be expected to demonstrate the terminal behavior in a real-life setting, and try to include as many of them in the objective as possible.

THE STANDARD WHICH WILL BE USED TO EVALUATE THE SUCCESS OF THE PRODUCT OR PERFORMANCE

We noted earlier in this volume that planning objectives provide information regarding *how effectively* a student must perform to demonstrate adequate mastery of a prescribed behavior. Readers also may recall that specifying the expected level of performance was one of the steps identified for formulating instructional objectives. In this section we discuss the relevant characteristics of standards required for determining the adequacy of responses.*

Definitions. *Standard* or *criterion* as used here refers to a basis for evaluating the prescribed behavior. Suppose you were told that you must throw a baseball fifty feet to perform the task successfully. The standard specified for determining whether you performed the task of throwing the baseball adequately was *fifty feet.*

A *performance standard,* then, is a specified level of achievement used to identify individuals who have mastered a task acceptably. *Achievement* here refers to performance in terms of its adequacy. We determine achievement by answering this question: "How effectively was a given task performed in respect to a specified criterion or standard?"

Several of the reasons for including performance standards in planning objectives were mentioned previously. Performance standards help both

*Matters related to test construction or preparing the means of evaluating whether objectives have been achieved are not examined in this book. There are a number of excellent books which the reader interested in educational measurement may wish to consult [Ebel, 1965; Horrocks, 1964; and Nunnally, 1964]. A recent measurement volume (Payne, 1968) with a primary emphasis on learning outcomes may be of particular interest to students concerned with the relationship between planning objectives and the measurement process.

teachers and students know where any given student is in any given program. They provide a minimal criterion and offer the potential of success to all students. Teachers find performance standards invaluable when preparing evaluative instruments and when determining the efficacy of their instructional programs. Mager (1962) indicates that when the minimum acceptable performance for each objective is specified we have a performance standard to use in assessing instructional programs.

Classes of Performance Standards. Various types of criteria may be used to determine mastery of given objectives. We will discuss some general types of performance standards as they relate to mastery level.

A specified level of mastery for objectives is generally determined arbitrarily and it may have a wide range. In one case the teacher may want the student to be able to list "all five steps similarly to the way they are stated in the textbook." In another case, the teacher may determine that, "given a 100-word typed message and five minutes in which to do the task, a student will type the message on a separate piece of paper; a successful, finished product will include no more than two errors (typing or any other kind of error)." In the latter case, the teacher has required almost perfect performance. (Although some typing teachers known to the authors would not agree that this criterion approximated perfect performance.)

Minimal mastery level refers to what a student has to do to "win the game" – to successfully achieve an objective. The typing objective described above asked for minimal mastery. For another example, consider the following phrase:

> . . . to be able to identify *at least five* characteristics of . . .

Identification of five characteristics is the minimal mastery level acceptable in that example.

It is not possible to specify all the criteria for mastery level here, because space is not available for a detailed discussion. However, here are some examples of different types of performance standards:

Minimum Number

". . . must list *four* steps. . . ."

". . . write all *ten words* presented accurately. . . ."

". . . distinguish *three* main ideas. . . ."

Percent or Proportion

"... write (spell) accurately *100 percent* of the 10 words presented. . . ."

"... list *80 percent* of the verbs appearing in a 200 word message . . . ."

Limitation of Departure from Fixed Standard

"... must be correct to the *nearest percent*. . . ."

"... must be within *five decibels* of. . . ."

Distinguishing Features of Successful Performance

"... the radio plays within a *one-day period*. . . ."

"... all balls on the paper are *colored red*. . . ."

Examples of constraints are used above to specify performance standards in planning objectives. They include limitations, restrictions, or confinements specifying or implying the conditions under which performance must occur to be successful. Consider the following example:

. . . to be able to walk a mile *within a ten minute period.*

The constraint or restriction is *within a ten minute period.* This phrase restricts the conditions (time limit) for successful terminal performance. One demonstrates mastery when one walks a mile "within a specified time period." Some examples of mastery level described above could be classified as constraints (*e.g.,* "... three out of four words. . . .", "... 80 percent. . . ."; "... must be correct to the nearest percent. . . .").

A potential point of confusion regarding constraints is related to the fact that they deal with conditions under which the behavior is to be demonstrated. In one sense, then, it is reasonable to classify such constraints under stimulus conditions which influence how the behavior will be executed satisfactorily. However, while constraints do specify limiting conditions regarding how the task is to be executed, the emphasis in using constraints as performance standards *is on how satisfactorily.* Note that the time-limit example above told the learner those conditions within which he must operate to master the objective.

Accuracy of Performance. Another matter related to standards borders on a semantic problem. Consider this example:

> Given 100 words presented orally by the teacher, the student will write down (spell) at least 80 percent of these words accurately. Accuracy will be determined by matching a student's responses on the written list to the correctly spelled words in the textbook (pp. x and y).

This objective has two standards worth distinguishing. The first standard, *"80 percent of these words,"* specifies the minimal level of mastery. The second standard states how the accuracy will be determined (*i.e.*, how accurate responses can be defined operationally, – "*Accuracy will be. . . the textbook (pp. x and y).*" Many writers of objectives specify the performance standard (how effective), but not *how* the accuracy of performance will be determined. We encourage you to include both of these types of standards in your planning objectives.

Suggestions to the Teacher. Two suggestions are offered to the teacher specifying performance standards.

1. Select carefully the actual criteria (and levels) for ascertaining mastery. Should you select criteria based on behavior levels which discriminate between successful and unsuccessful performance? Should you specify criteria low enough for everyone to get over them easily (which will make you look like a great instructor), or high enough so that only the most able can master the performance standard (which will probably make you look like a poor teacher)?

2. Use a variety of measures, and where possible, describe alternative means for evaluating objectives. For some objectives, various behaviors such as "to identify" or "to distinguish" could be required for the same or similar material to be mastered. Why not change the level of the performance standard according to the task?

DIFFICULTIES ENCOUNTERED IN SPECIFYING PLANNING OBJECTIVES

Problems will be encountered as you specify planning objectives. We have identified a few of these difficulties so you may be alert for them as you formulate this type of objective. Some of the problems identified here first were encountered in a thoughtful report prepared by Ammerman and Melching (1966).

Sometimes an instructor fails to specify important performance standards because the information is not readily available for an instructional decision. Be careful not to be satisfied with less important objectives just because measuring devices are available or because certain behaviors are easy to measure. If a complex learning operation is important but not included in an objective, break it down into its component parts and develop standards to assess the level of mastery of each part. If we do not have standards for successful performance we should begin developing them, and now is as good a time as any.

Another potential difficulty is associated with utility. What is the mastery for? While it may be convenient to measure whether three out of four steps of x process are included in a written statement, maybe all four steps must be demonstrated to actually use the process; mastery of three steps may be of little or no value. Moreover, the value of mastery becomes even more clear when the total process of learning is considered. Today's planning objectives are used to create tomorrow's pre-instructional evaluation for the next higher level of instruction.

A problem somewhat related to utility is making the objectives relevant to the task (*i.e.,* derived from the known work requirements for a given job or learning task). Those activities which students are required to engage in that are not required to be performed in a work situation or in a higher order learning level may be of limited value. There is also the possibility of stating planning objectives (and particularly performance standards) which are related primarily to a testing situation, rather than to the next set or ultimate learning operation to be acquired.

Still another problem is related to the teacher knowing what objectives he wants to achieve and communicating his knowledge to the student. If the instructor has not specified planning objectives, one could infer that he has not decided what students should be able to do as a result of instruction. Missing performance standards or other incomplete information in planning objectives invite similar inferences from outside observers like colleagues, parents, and administrators.

A difficult but important task for the teacher is to arrange planning objectives, and performance standards for given planning objectives, into a priority. It is critical to learning to arrange the priorities for given tasks into an efficient order to increase learning. It is just as important to arrange the priority of performance standards (and to use several of them) to determine the mastery required for a given objective.

CHAPTER III

Objectives and the Behavioral Domains

In attempting to specify and measure instructional objectives, it is usually desirable to determine the classes of behaviors reflected in the objectives. Teachers and researchers have found it useful to classify objectives into cognitive, affective, and psychomotor domains. The major reasons for classifying objectives are (1) to avoid concentrating on one or two categories to the exclusion of others, (2) to make sure that instruction is provided for prerequisite objectives before attempting to teach more complex ones, and (3) to assure that appropriate instruments are employed to evaluate desired objectives.

Some objectives include more than one behavioral domain. For example, an objective such as "to be able to present an original five-minute speech in front of the class without exhibiting stage fright" includes as many as three different domains of human behavior. The first class of behaviors implied in this objective is psychomotor skills involved in meaningful sound production; the second behavioral class involves attitudes toward the speaking situation, or affective behaviors. The objective also assumes that the student is capable of comprehending and repeating information contained in the speech (cognitive behaviors). Thus, what on the surface appears to be a simple objective of instruction involves several different classes or domains of behavior. Moreover, some classes of behavior are easier to evaluate than others. The psychomotor and cognitive aspects of the above objective would be considerably easier to evaluate objectively than the aspects dealing with attitudes.

The three behavioral domains mentioned above still represent only broad classifications of human behavior and educational objectives. Within each of these behavioral areas it is possible to classify objectives into progressive levels of development. Bloom and others (1956) and Krathwohl and others (1964) have conducted a systematic survey of educational objectives in the cognitive and affective domains and have prepared taxonomies for these two classes of behavior. The taxonomies evolved as a result of a 1948 meeting of university examiners and scholars interested in test development and construction at an American Psychological Association Convention in Boston. The taxonomies were prepared in response to a need expressed by members of this group for standardized terminology regarding human behavioral characteristics which educators attempt to appraise.

Educators often are faced with the problem of interpreting abstract terms such as *like, appreciate, value, understand, enjoy,* and *know.* In the statement, "I want my students to enjoy classical music," it is unclear whether the author of the objective wants students to (1) listen to the music without throwing paper wads at other students, (2) go out and buy a classical record as a result of the course, (3) have a "deep emotional reaction" to a given piece of music, or (4) change one's major area of study to classical music. This wide range of possible variations and subsequent interpretations among educators regarding abstract objectives provided an additional stimulus for the development of the taxonomies. The taxonomies provide a framework for specifying specific objectives as well as an alternative to the common abstract statements concerning instructional goals.

It is reasonable to question the rationale for classifying rather complex behaviors into simple behavioral domains. Bloom and others (1956) suggested at least four values which provide the rationale for their taxonomies:

1. "To help clarify and tighten language of educational objectives"
2. "To provide a convenient system for describing and ordering test items, examination techniques, and evaluation instruments"
3. "To provide a framework for comparing and studying educational programs"
4. "To discover some of the principles of ordering human-learning outcomes. . .that a useful theory of learning must be able to explain."

The comittee responsible for the development of the taxonomies believed that these values were important enough to overcome the obvious pitfalls associated with arbitrarily classifying objectives into apparently discrete domains.

INTERRELATIONSHIPS AMONG THE THREE BEHAVIORAL DOMAINS

As the example at the beginning of this chapter illustrates, it is often difficult to isolate the behavioral domains present in a given objective. In fact, one of the major drawbacks of the taxonomy of behaviors is the tendency to place a specific objective in one behavioral domain when it more properly should be placed in two or more of the domains. This weakness of classification systems has long been recognized. We are all familiar with the attacks by general semanticists on Aristotle for attempting to classify matter into discrete units. However, Aristotle's classifications still exist as do others in physical, biological, and social sciences as well as in education. The pragmatic values of such classification schemes often outweigh the drawbacks.

Although educators accept the fact that affective, cognitive, and psychomotor skills are interrelated highly in many areas, it often is necessary to emphasize one of the areas to the exclusion of the others in order to measure achievement of desired skills objectively. For example, an objective "to be able to recite the Preamble to the Constitution in front of the class" generally would be placed in the cognitive domain. An educator attempting to measure this objective would no doubt listen as the student recites and note the accuracy of the recitation. However, the underlying reason for having a child recite the Preamble to the Constitution also, no doubt, would involve a less clearly defined set of objectives relating to the formation of positive attitudes towards one's cultural heritage and, specifically, one's government. These objectives relating to the affective domain would be much more difficult to measure objectively and, therefore, might be overlooked or never recognized consciously. Since recitation involves the physiological act of speech, there are also objectives related to the psychomotor domain subsumed under the original objectives. These could be measured by the instructor, if desired, but usually would not be emphasized or would be taken for granted.

Thus, even though it is virtually impossible to isolate the three behavioral domains in practice, there is still some justification for placing an objective in one of three categories from a practical viewpoint. Educators should be aware that making such arbitrary classifications of objectives could lead potentially to emphases in learning which are not necessarily most important. They should, therefore, view the following classifications of objectives with some caution.

A useful system for writing objectives for the cognitive and affective domains has been developed recently by Metfessel, Michael and Kirsner (1969). A report of their work is included in Appendix C for the benefit of interested readers.

COGNITIVE DOMAIN

When developing the taxonomies, Bloom's committee found that the majority of objectives in the educational literature was related to the cognitive domain. The objectives classified as cognitive emphasize intellectual, learning, and problem solving tasks. Behaviors in this domain range from performing simple recall tasks to placing previously learned material into new contexts and synthesizing bodies of learned information. The following abstract of the taxonomy of educational objectives for the cognitive domain indicates the levels of cognitive behaviors under which objectives may be classified, provides brief definitions for each level, and, in most cases, provides sample objectives for the specific levels of behavior.

A CONDENSED VERSION OF THE COGNITIVE DOMAIN OF THE TAXONOMY OF EDUCATIONAL OBJECTIVES*

KNOWLEDGE

1.00 KNOWLEDGE

Knowledge, as defined here, involves the recall of specifics and universals, the recall of methods and processes, or the recall of a

*From David R. Krathwohl, Benjamin S. Bloom and Bertram B. Masia, *Taxonomy of Educational Objectives – The Classification of Educational Goals, Handbook II: Affective Domain.* New York: David McKay Co., Inc., 1964, pp. 186-193. Reprinted by permission David McKay Co., Inc. (This is an abstract of *Taxonomy of Educational Objectives – The Classification of Educational Goals, Handbook I: Cognitive Domain* by Benjamin S. Bloom, et al., New York: David McKay Co., Inc., 1956.)

pattern, structure, or setting. For measurement purposes, the recall situation involves little more than bringing to mind the appropriate material. Although some alteration of the material may be required, this is a relatively minor part of the task. The knowledge objectives emphasize most the psychological processes of remembering. The process of relating is also involved in that a knowledge test situation requires the organization and reorganization of a problem such that it will furnish the appropriate signals and cues for the information and knowledge the individual possesses. To use an analogy, if one thinks of the mind as a file, the problem in a knowledge test situation is that of finding in the problem or task the appropriate signals, cues, and clues which will most effectively bring out whatever knowledge is filed or stored.

1.10 Knowledge of Specifics

The recall of specific and isolable bits of information. The emphasis is on symbols with concrete referents. This material, which is at a very low level of abstraction, may be thought of as the elements from which more complex and abstract forms of knowledge are built.

1.11 Knowledge of Terminology. Knowledge of the referents for specific symbols (verbal and nonverbal). This may include knowledge of the most generally accepted symbol referent, knowledge of the variety of symbols which may be used for a single referent, or knowledge of the referent most appropriate to a given use of a symbol.

To define technical terms by giving their attributes, properties, or relations.

Familiarity with a large number of words in their common range of meanings.*

1.12 Knowledge of Specific Facts. Knowledge of dates, events, persons, places, etc. This may include very precise and specific information such as the specific date or exact magnitude of a

*Each subcategory is followed by illustrative educational objectives selected from the literature.

phenomenon. It may also include approximate or relative information such as an approximate time period or the general order of magnitude of a phenomenon.

The recall of major facts about particular cultures.

The possession of a minimum knowledge about the organisms studied in the laboratory.

1.20 Knowledge of Ways and Means of Dealing With Specifics

Knowledge of the ways of organizing, studying, judging, and criticizing. This includes the methods of inquiry, the chronological sequences, and the standards of judgment within a field as well as the patterns of organization through which the areas of the fields themselves are determined and internally organized. This knowledge is at an intermediate level of abstraction between specific knowledge on the one hand and knowledge of universals on the other. It does not so much demand the activity of the student in using the materials as it does a more passive awareness of their nature.

1.21 Knowledge of Conventions. Knowledge of characteristic ways of treating and presenting ideas and phenomena. For purposes of communication and consistency, workers in a field employ usages, styles, practices, and forms which best suit their purposes and/or which appear to suit best the phenomena with which they deal. It should be recognized that although these forms and conventions are likely to be set up on arbitrary, accidental, or authoritative bases, they are retained because of the general agreement or concurrence of individuals concerned with the subject, phenomena, or problem.

Familiarity with the forms and conventions of the major types of works; *e.g.*, verse, plays, scientific papers, etc.

To make pupils conscious of correct form and usage in speech and writing.

1.22 Knowledge of Trends and Sequences. Knowledge of the processes, directions, and movements of phenomena with respect to time.

Understanding of the continuity and development of American culture as exemplified in American life.

Knowledge of the basic trends underlying the development of public assistance programs.

1.23 Knowledge of Classifications and Categories. Knowledge of the classes, sets, divisions, and arrangements which are regarded as fundamental for a given subject field, purpose, argument, or problem.

To recognize the area encompassed by various kinds of problems or materials.

Becoming familiar with a range of types of literature.

1.24 Knowledge of Criteria. Knowledge of the criteria by which facts, principles, opinions, and conduct are tested or judged.

Familiarity with criteria for judgment appropriate to the type of work and the purpose for which it is read.

Knowledge of criteria for the evaluation of recreational activities.

1.25 Knowledge of Methodology. Knowledge of the methods of inquiry, techniques, and procedures employed in a particular subject field as well as those employed in investigating particular problems and phenomena. The emphasis here is on the individual's knowledge of the method rather than his ability to use the method.

Knowledge of scientific methods for evaluating health concepts.

The student shall know the methods of attack relevant to the kinds of problems of concern to the social sciences.

1.30 Knowledge of the Universals and Abstractions in a Field.

Knowledge of the major schemes and patterns by which phenomena and ideas are organized. These are the large structures, theories, and generalizations which dominate a subject field or which are quite generally used in studying phenomena or solving problems. These are at the highest levels of abstraction and complexity.

1.31 Knowledge of Principles and Generalizations. Knowledge of particular abstractions which summarize observations of phenomena. These are the abstractions which are of value in explaining, describing, predicting, or in determining the most appropriate and relevant action or direction to be taken.

Knowledge of the important principles by which our experience with biological phenomena is summarized.
The recall of major generalizations about particular cultures.

1.32 Knowledge of Theories and Structures. Knowledge of the *body* of principles and generalizations together with their interrelations which present a clear, rounded, and systematic view of a complex phenomenon, problem, or field. These are the most abstract formulations, and they can be used to show the interrelation and organization of a great range of specifics.

The recall of major theories about particular cultures.
Knowledge of a relatively complete formulation of the theory of evolution.

INTELLECTUAL ABILITIES AND SKILLS

Abilities and skills refer to organized modes of operation and generalized techniques for dealing with materials and problems. The materials and problems may be of such a nature that little or no specialized and technical information is required. Such information as is required can be assumed to be part of the individual's general fund of knowledge. Other problems may require specialized and technical information at a rather high level such that specific knowledge and skill in dealing with the problem and the materials are required. The abilities and skills objectives emphasize the mental processes of organizing and reorganizing material to achieve a particular purpose. The materials may be given or remembered.

2.00 COMPREHENSION

This represents the lowest level of understanding. It refers to a type of understanding or apprehension such that the individual knows what is being communicated and can make use of the material or idea being communicated without necessarily relating it to other material or seeing its fullest implications.

2.10 Translation

Comprehension as evidenced by the care and accuracy with which the communication is paraphrased or rendered from one language or form of communication to another. Translation is judged on the basis of faithfulness and accuracy; that is, on the extent to which the material in the original communication is preserved although the form of the communication has been altered.

The ability to understand nonliteral statements (metaphor, symbolism, irony, exaggeration).

Skill in translating mathematical verbal material into symbolic statements and vice versa.

2.20 Interpretation

The explanation or summarization of a communication. Whereas translation involves an objective part-for-part rendering of a communication, interpretation involves a reordering, rearrangement, or new view of the material.

The ability to grasp the thought of the work as a whole at any desired level of generality.

The ability to interpret various types of social data.

2.30 Extrapolation

The extension of trends or tendencies beyond the given data to determine implications, consequences, corollaries, effects, etc., which are in accordance with the conditions described in the original communication.

The ability to deal with the conclusions of a work in terms of the immediate inference made from the explicit statements.

Skill in predicting continuation of trends.

3.00 APPLICATION

The use of abstractions in particular and concrete situations. The abstractions may be in the form of general ideas, rules of procedures, or generalized methods. The abstractions may also be technical principles, ideas, and theories which must be remembered and applied.

Application to the phenomena discussed in one paper of the scientific terms or concepts used in other papers.

The ability to predict the probable effect of a change in a factor on a biological situation previously at equilibrium.

4.00 ANALYSIS

The breakdown of a communication into its constituent elements or parts such that the relative hierarchy of ideas is made clear and/or the relations between the ideas expressed are made explicit. Such analyses are intended to clarify the communication, to indicate how the communication is organized, and the way in which it manages to convey its effects, as well as its basis and arrangement.

4.10 Analysis of Elements

Identification of the elements included in a communication.

The ability to recognize unstated assumptions.

Skill in distinguishing facts from hypotheses.

4.20 Analysis of Relationships

The connections and interactions between elements and parts of a communication.

Ability to check the consistency of hypotheses with given information and assumptions.

Skill in comprehending the interrelationships among the ideas in a passage.

4.30 Analysis of Organizational Principles

The organization, systematic arrangement, and structure which hold the communication together. This includes the "explicit" as well as "implicit" structure. It includes the bases, necessary arrangement, and mechanics which make the communication a unit.

The ability to recognize form and pattern in literary or artistic works as a means of understanding their meaning.

Ability to recognize the general techniques used in persuasive materials, such as advertising, propaganda, etc.

5.00 SYNTHESIS

The putting together of elements and parts so as to form a whole. This involves the process of working with pieces, parts, elements, etc., and arranging and combining them in such a way as to constitute a pattern or structure not clearly there before.

5.10 Production of a Unique Communication

The development of a communication in which the writer or speaker attempts to convey ideas, feelings, and/or experiences to others.

Skill in writing, using an excellent organization of ideas and statements.

Ability to tell a personal experience effectively.

5.20 Production of a Plan, or Proposed Set of Operations

The development of a plan of work or the proposal of a plan of operations. The plan should satisfy requirements of the task which may be given to the student or which he may develop for himself.

Ability to propose ways of testing hypotheses.

Ability to plan a unit of instruction for a particular teaching situation.

5.30 Derivation of a Set of Abstract Relations

The development of a set of abstract relations either to classify or explain particular data or phenomena, or the deduction of propositions and relations from a set of basic propositions or symbolic representations.

Ability to formulate appropriate hypotheses based upon an analysis of factors involved, and to modify such hypotheses in the light of new factors and considerations.

Ability to make mathematical discoveries and generalizations.

6.00 EVALUATION

Judgments about the value of material and methods for given purposes. Quantitative and qualitative judgments about the extent to which material and methods satisfy criteria. Use of a standard of appraisal. The criteria may be those determined by the student or those which are given to him.

6.10 Judgments in Terms of Internal Evidence

Evaluation of the accuracy of a communication from such evidence as logical accuracy, consistency, and other internal criteria.

Judging by internal standards, the ability to assess general probability of accuracy in reporting facts from the care given to exactness of statement, documentation, proof, etc.

The ability to indicate logical fallacies in arguments.

6.20 Judgments in Terms of External Criteria

Evaluation of material with reference to selected or remembered criteria.

The comparison of major theories, generalizations, and facts about particular cultures.

Judging by external standards, the ability to compare a work with the highest known standards in its field – especially with other works of recognized excellence.

AFFECTIVE DOMAIN

The second largest number of objectives found in the educational literature could be placed into one of the levels of the affective domain.

The taxonomy committee found it more difficult to determine a hierarchial order of affective behaviors. The affective domain contains behaviors and objectives which have some emotional overtone. It encompasses likes and dislikes, attitudes, values and beliefs. The following is an abstract of the taxonomy of educational objectives for the affective domain.

A CONDENSED VERSION OF THE AFFECTIVE DOMAIN OF THE TAXONOMY OF EDUCATIONAL OBJECTIVES*

1.0 RECEIVING (ATTENDING)

At this level we are concerned that the learner be sensitized to the existence of certain phenomena and stimuli; that is, that he be willing to receive or to attend to them. This is clearly the first and crucial step if the learner is to be properly oriented to learn what the teacher intends that he will. To indicate that this is the bottom rung of the ladder, however, is not at all to imply that the teacher is starting *de novo.* Because of previous experience (formal or informal), the student brings to each situation a point of view or set which may facilitate or hinder his recognition of the phenomena to which the teacher is trying to sensitize him.

The category of *Receiving* has been divided into three subcategories to indicate three different levels of attending to phenomena. While the division points between the subcategories are arbitrary, the subcategories do represent a continuum. From an extremely passive position or role on the part of the learner, where the sole responsibility for the evocation of the behavior rests with the teacher – that is, the responsibility rests with him for "capturing" the student's attention – the continuum extends to a point at which the learner directs his attention, at least at a semiconscious level, toward the preferred stimuli.

*David R. Krathwohl, Benjamin S. Bloom, and Bertram B. Masia, *Taxonomy of Educational Objectives – The Classification of Educational Goals, Handbook II: Affective Domain.* New York: David McKay Co., Inc., 1964, pp. 176-185. Reprinted by permission David McKay Co., Inc.

1.1 Awareness

Awareness is almost a cognitive behavior. But unlike *Knowledge,* the lowest level of the cognitive domain, we are not so much concerned with a memory of, or ability to recall, an item or fact as we are that, given appropriate opportunity, the learner will merely be conscious of something – that he take into account a situation, phenomenon, object, or stage of affairs. Like *Knowledge* it does not imply an assessment of the qualities or nature of the stimulus, but unlike *Knowledge* it does not necessarily imply attention. There can be simple awareness without specific discrimination or recognition of the objective characteristics of the object, even though these characteristics must be deemed to have an effect. The individual may not be able to verbalize the aspects of the stimulus which cause the awareness.

Develops awareness of aesthetic factors in dress, furnishings, architecture, city design, good art, and the like.

Develops some consciousness of color, form, arrangement, and design in the objects and structures around him and in descriptive or symbolic representations of people, things, and situations.*

1.2 Willingness to Receive

In this category we have come a step up the ladder but are still dealing with what appears to be cognitive behavior. At a minimum level, we are here describing the behavior of being willing to tolerate a given stimulus, not to avoid it. Like *Awareness,* it involves a neutrality or suspended judgment toward the stimulus. At this level of the continuum the teacher is not concerned that the student seek it out, nor even, perhaps, that in an environment crowded with many other stimuli the learner will necessarily attend to the stimulus. Rather, at worst, given the opportunity to attend in a field with relatively few competing stimuli, the learner is not actively seeking to avoid it. At best, he is willing to take notice of the phenomenon and give it his attention.

*Illustrative objectives selected from the literature follow the description of each subcategory.

Attends (carefully) when others speak – in direct conversation, on the telephone, in audiences.

Appreciation (tolerance) of cultural patterns exhibited by individuals from other groups – religious, social, political, economic, national, etc.

Increase in sensitivity to human need and pressing social problems.

1.3 Controlled or Selected Attention

At a somewhat higher level we are concerned with a new phenomenon, the differentiation of a given stimulus into figure and ground at a conscious or perhaps semiconscious level – the differentiation of aspects of a stimulus which is perceived as clearly marked off from adjacent impressions. The perception is still without tension or assessment, and the student may not know the technical terms or symbols with which to describe it correctly or precisely to others. In some instances it may refer not so much to the selectivity of attention as to the control of attention, so that when certain stimuli are present they will be attended to. There is an element of the learner's controlling the attention here, so that the favored stimulus is selected and attended to despite competing and distracting stimuli.

Listens to music with some discrimination as to its mood and meaning and with some recognition of the contributions of various musical elements and instruments to the total effect.

Alertness toward human values and judgments on life as they are recorded in literature.

2.0 RESPONDING

At this level we are concerned with responses which go beyond merely attending to the phenomenon. The student is sufficiently motivated that he is not just 1.2 *Willing to attend,* but perhaps it is correct to say that he is actively attending. As a first stage in a "learning by doing" process the student is committing himself in some small measure to the phenomena involved. This is a very low level of commitment, and we would not say at this level that this was "a value of his" or that he had "such and such an attitude." These terms belong to the next higher level that we describe. But we could say that he is doing something with or about the phenomenon besides merely perceiving it, as would be true at the next level below this of 1.3 *Controlled or selected attention.*

This is the category that many teachers will find best describes their "interest" objectives. Most commonly we use the term to indicate the desire that a child become sufficiently involved in or committed to a subject, phenomenon, or activity that he will seek it out and gain satisfaction from working with it or engaging in it.

2.1 Acquiescence in Responding

We might use the word "obedience" or "compliance" to describe this behavior. As both of these terms indicate, there is a passiveness so far as the initiation of the behavior is concerned, and the stimulus calling for this behavior is not subtle. Compliance is perhaps a better term than obedience, since there is more of the element of reaction to a suggestion and less of the implication of resistance or yielding unwillingly. The student makes the response, but he has not fully accepted the necessity for doing so.

Willingness to comply with health regulations.
Obeys the playground regulations.

2.2 Willingness to Respond

The key to this level is in the term "willingness," with its implication of capacity for voluntary activity. There is the implication that the learner is sufficiently committed to exhibiting the behavior that he does so not just because of a fear of punishment, but "on his own" or voluntarily. It may help to note that the element of resistance or of yielding unwillingly, which is possibly present at the previous level, is here replaced with consent or proceeding from one's own choice.

Acquaints himself with significant current issues in international, political, social, and economic affairs through voluntary reading and discussion.

Acceptance of responsibility for his own health and for the protection of the health of others.

2.3 Satisfaction in Response

The additional element in the step beyond the *Willingness to respond* level, the consent, the assent to responding, or the voluntary response, is that the behavior is accompanied by a feeling of satisfaction, an emotional response, generally of pleasure, zest, or enjoyment. The location of this category in the hierarchy has given us a great deal of difficulty. Just where in the process of internalization the attachment of an emotional response, kick, or thrill to a behavior occurs has been hard to determine. For that matter there is some uncertainty as to whether the level of internalization at which it occurs may not depend on the particular behavior. We have even questioned whether it should be a category. If our structure is to be a hierarchy, then each category should include the behavior in the next level below it. The emotional component appears gradually through the range of internalization categories. The attempt to specify a given position in the hierarchy as *the* one at which the emotional component is added is doomed to failure.

The category is arbitrarily placed at this point in the hierarchy where it seems to appear most frequently and where it is cited as, or appears to be, an important component of the objectives at this level on the continuum. The category's inclusion at this point serves the pragmatic purpose of reminding us of the presence of the emotional component and its value in the building of affective behaviors. But it should not be thought of as appearing and occurring at this one point in the continuum and thus destroying the hierarchy which we are attempting to build.

Enjoyment of self-expression in music and in arts and crafts as another means of personal enrichment.

Finds pleasure in reading for recreation.

Takes pleasure in conversing with many different kinds of people.

3.0 VALUING

This is the only category headed by a term which is in common use in the expression of objectives by teachers. Further, it is employed in its usual sense: that a thing, phenomenon, or behavior has worth. This abstract concept of worth is in part a result of the individual's own valuing or assessment, but it is much more a social product that has been slowly internalized or accepted and has come to be used by the student as his own criterion of worth.

Behavior categorized at this level is sufficiently consistent and stable to have taken on the characteristics of a belief or an attitude. The learner displays this behavior with sufficient consistency in appropriate situations that he comes to be perceived as holding a value. At this level, we are not concerned with the relationships among values but rather with the internalization of a set of specified, ideal, values. Viewed from another standpoint, the objectives classified here are the prime stuff from which the conscience of the individual is developed into active control of behavior.

This category will be found appropriate for many objectives that use the term "attitude" (as well as, of course, "value").

An important element of behavior characterized by *Valuing* is that it is motivated, not by the desire to comply or obey, but by the individual's commitment to the underlying value guiding the behavior.

3.1 Acceptance of a Value

At this level we are concerned with the ascribing of worth to a phenomenon, behavior, object, etc. The term "belief," which is defined as "the emotional acceptance of a proposition or doctrine upon what one implicitly considers adequate ground" (English and English, 1958, p. 64), describes quite well what may be thought of as the dominant characteristic here. Beliefs have varying degrees of certitude. At this lowest level of *Valuing* we are concerned with the lowest levels of certainty; that is, there is more of a readiness to re-evaluate one's position than at the higher levels. It is a position that is somewhat tentative.

One of the distinguishing characteristics of this behavior is consistency of response to the class of objects, phenomena, etc., with which the belief or attitude is identified. It is consistent enough so that the person is perceived by others as holding the belief or value. At the level we are describing here, he is both sufficiently consistent that others can identify the value, and sufficiently committed that he is willing to be so identified.

Continuing desire to develop the ability to speak and write effectively.

Grows in his sense of kinship with human beings of all nations.

3.2 Preference for a Value

The provision for this subdivision arose out of a feeling that there were objectives that expressed a level of internalization between the mere acceptance of a value and commitment or conviction in the usual connotation of deep involvement in an area. Behavior at this level implies not just the acceptance of a value to the point of being willing to be identified with it, but the individual is sufficiently committed to the value to pursue it, to seek it out, to want it.

Assumes responsibility for drawing reticent members of a group into conversation.

Deliberately examines a variety of viewpoints on controversial issues with a view to forming opinions about them.

Actively participates in arranging for the showing of contemporary artistic efforts.

3.3 Commitment

Belief at this level involves a high degree of certainty. The ideas of "conviction" and "certainty beyond a shadow of a doubt" help to convey further the level of behavior intended. In some instances this may border on faith, in the sense of it being a firm emotional acceptance of a belief upon admittedly nonrational grounds. Loyalty to a position, group, or cause would also be classified here.

The person who displays behavior at this level is clearly perceived as holding the value. He acts to further the thing valued in some way, to extend the possibility of his developing it, to deepen his involvement with it and with the things representing it. He tries to convince others and seeks converts to his cause. There is a tension here which needs to be satisfied; action is the result of an aroused need or drive. There is a real motivation to act out the behavior.

Devotion to those ideas and ideals which are the foundations of democracy.

Faith in the power of reason and in methods of experiment and discussion.

4.0 ORGANIZATION

As the learner successively internalizes values, he encounters situations for which more than one value is relevant. Thus necessity arises for (a) the organization of the values into a system, (b) the determination of the interrelationships among them, and (c) the establishment of the dominant and pervasive ones. Such a system is built gradually, subject to change as new values are incorporated. This category is intended as the proper classification for objectives which describe the beginnings of the building of a value system. It is subdivided into two levels, since a prerequisite to interrelating is the conceptualization of the value in a form which permits organization. *Conceptualization* forms the first subdivision in the organization process, *Organization of a value system* the second.

While the order of the two subcategories seems appropriate enough with reference to one another, it is not so certain that 4.1 *Conceptualization of a value* is properly placed as the next level above 3.3 *Commitment.* Conceptualization undoubtedly begins at an earlier level for some objectives. Like 2.3 *Satisfaction in response,* it is doubtful that a single completely satisfactory location for this category can be found. Positioning it before 4.2 *Organization of a value system* appropriately indicates a prerequisite of such a system. It also calls attention to a component of affective growth that occurs at least by this point on the continuum but may begin earlier.

4.1 Conceptualization of a Value

In the previous category, 3.0 *Valuing,* we noted that consistency and stability are integral characteristics of the particular value or belief. At this level (4.1) the quality of abstraction or conceptualization is added. This permits the individual to see how the value relates to those that he already holds or to new ones that he is coming to hold.

Conceptualization will be abstract, and in this sense it will be symbolic. But the symbols need not be verbal symbols. Whether conceptualization first appears at this point on the affective continuum is a moot point, as noted above.

Attempts to identify the characteristics of an art object which he admires.

Forms judgments as to the responsibility of society for conserving human and material resources.

4.2 Organization of a Value System

Objectives properly classified here are those which require the learner to bring together a complex of values, possibly disparate values, and to bring these into an ordered relationship with one another. Ideally, the ordered relationship will be one which is harmonious and internally consistent. This is, of course, the goal of such objectives, which seek to have the student formulate a philosophy of life. In actuality, the integration may be something less than entirely harmonious. More likely the relationship is better described as a kind of dynamic equilibrium which is, in part, dependent upon those portions of the environment which are salient at any point in time. In many instances the organization of values may result in their synthesis into a new value or value complex of a higher order.

Weighs alternative social policies and practices against the standards of the public welfare rather than the advantage of specialized and narrow interest groups.

Develops a plan for regulating his rest in accordance with the demands of his activities.

5.0 CHARACTERIZATION BY A VALUE OR VALUE COMPLEX

At this level of internalization the values already have a place in the individual's value hierarchy, are organized into some kind of internally consistent system, have controlled the behavior of the individual for a sufficient time that he has adapted to behaving this way; and an evocation of the behavior no longer arouses emotion or affect except when the individual is threatened or challenged.

The individual acts consistently in accordance with the values he has internalized at this level, and our concern is to indicate two things: (a) the generalization of this control to so much of the individual's behavior that he is described and characterized as a person by these pervasive controlling tendencies, and (b) the integration of these beliefs, ideas, and attitudes into a total philosophy or world view. These two aspects constitute the subcategories.

5.1 Generalized Set

The generalized set is that which gives an internal consistency to the system of attitudes and values at any particular moment. It is selective responding at a very high level. It is sometimes spoken of as a determining tendency, an orientation toward phenomena, or a predisposition to act in a certain way. The generalized set is a response to highly generalized phenomena. It is a persistent and consistent response to a family of related situations or objects. It may often be an unconscious set which guides action without conscious forethought. The generalized set may be thought of as closely related to the idea of an attitude cluster, where the commonality is based on behavioral characteristics rather than the subject or object of the attitude. A generalized set is a basic orientation which enables the individual to reduce and order the complex world about him and to act consistently and effectively in it.

Readiness to revise judgments and to change behavior in the light of evidence.

Judges problems and issues in terms of situations, issues, purposes, and consequences involved rather than in terms of fixed, dogmatic precepts or emotionally wishful thinking.

5.2 Characterization

This, the peak of the internalization process, includes those objectives which are broadest with respect both to the phenomena covered and to the range of behavior which they comprise. Thus, here are found those objectives which concern one's view of the universe, one's philosophy of life, one's *Weltanschauung*– a value system having as its object the whole of what is known or knowable.

Objectives categorized here are more than generalized sets in the sense that they involve a greater inclusiveness and, within the group of attitudes, behaviors, beliefs, or ideas, an emphasis on internal consistency. Though this internal consistency may not always be exhibited behaviorally by the students toward whom the objective is directed, since we are categorizing teachers' objectives, this consistency feature will always be a component of *Characterization* objectives.

As the title of the category implies, these objectives are so encompassing that they tend to characterize the individual almost completely.

Develops for regulation of one's personal and civic life a code of behavior based on ethical principles consistent with democratic ideals.

Develops a consistent philosophy of life.

PSYCHOMOTOR DOMAIN

Few objectives in the psychomotor domain were found in the educational literature. Consequently, the taxonomy committee decided to withold further work on the project until more attention was directed toward this domain by curriculum planners and educators. The few objectives which have appeared in the literature primarily have involved speech and writing skills, craft and woodworking skills, music and other performance arts, and athletic skills.

The authors of the present volume, viewing a need to begin the systematic classification of psychomotor behaviors, have formulated a set of subclassifications of behaviors in the psychomotor domain. The classifications are *not* intended to represent a taxonomy. That is, they do not necessarily represent a hierarchy of skills in the psychomotor domain. Further refinement and analysis by other educators eventually may yield a taxonomic structure from the classifications listed below. The purposes for making classifications at this point are (1) to provide a framework for examining a variety of psychomotor objectives, and (2) to provide initial definitions for classes of psychomotor behavior.

Psychomotor skills frequently have been labeled "motor" skills and "perceptual-motor" skills in educational and psychological literature. Tasks involving psychomotor skills have been defined by Noble (1968) in the following manner:

> . . . psychomotor skill tasks are those situations that require the identification and combination of stimulus-organism-response elements into coordinated spatiotemporal patterns of receptor-effector activity as a joint function of practice repetitions and reinforcing feedback so as to optimize probability, amplitude, and time scores in acquisition, retention, and transfer. (p. 203)

This definition, although more technical than the scope of this book demands, will serve as the basis for discriminating those behaviors which will be included in the psychomotor domain.

The authors prefer to subdivide the psychomotor domain into behaviors involving (1) gross bodily movements, (2) finely coordinated bodily movements, (3) non-verbal communication behaviors, and (4) speech behaviors.

These categories were derived, in part, from theory and research in child development. Research indicates and observation confirms that children first develop gross movements, such as kicking, rolling over, and sitting, before they develop finely coordinated skills, such as manipulating objects and playing games involving hand-eye coordination. Similarly, communication on a nonverbal basis (*e.g.*, via gestures) generally precedes oral communication. Meaningful sound (speech) production generally develops after nonverbal communicative behaviors have been refined. With this child development model in mind, the authors have established these four general categories of psychomotor skills, realizing that some of the skills may overlap among classifications. Sample objectives are provided for each section.

CLASSIFICATION OF PSYCHOMOTOR BEHAVIOR

1.00 GROSS BODILY MOVEMENTS

Behaviors in this category are characterized by movements of entire limbs in isolation or in conjunction with other parts of the body. The movements may be performed by a person alone, by a person in conjunction with another object, or between two or more persons. Although some coordination of movements with the eye or ear are obviously necessary, primary emphases usually are on strength, speed, or precision in objectives involving gross movements. Objectives which primarily are dependent upon coordination with eye or ear are placed in the second category (2.00) of psychomotor skills.

1.10 Movements Involving the Upper Limbs

Objectives in this category are related primarily to behaviors focusing on the use of arms and shoulders, such as throwing, catching, and pulling oneself up.

To be able to throw a baseball 35 feet.
To be able to do 10 chin-ups.

1.20 Lower Limbs

Objectives in this classification focus primarily on the use of feet and legs. Behaviors which would fall in this class include such activities as running, jumping, marching, and kicking.

To be able to run the 100 yard dash in 15 seconds.

To be able to march around the room three times in step to a military march.

To be able to raise and lower the right leg 10 times in succession from a prone position to a 45-degree angle.

1.30 Movements Involving Two or More Bodily Units

The behaviors represented by objectives in this class involve a combination of arm and leg movements or of movements using the entire body. Examples of activities in this behavioral class are swimming, diving, gymnastics, and dancing.

To be able to swim 100 yards using the Australian crawl.

To be able to execute a 1½ gainer with an average rating of 5.5 (on a 10-point scale) by a panel of three expert judges.

To be able to execute the five basic ballet positions with a minimum rating of 5, by two or three judges (on a 7-point scale).

2.00 FINELY COORDINATED MOVEMENTS

Behaviors in this classification primarily involve coordinated movements of the extremities, usually in conjunction with the eye or ear. The emphasis is on a pattern or sequence of coordinated movements, usually in combination with some external object. Objectives in this area may be found in fine arts, handicraft, woodworking (industrial arts), applied music, recreation, commercial arts, and written communication, to name but a few.

The behaviors in this class are often produced through a conditioning process. Measurements of these behaviors often represent an attempt to assess the degree of conditioning which has occurred at a given point in time. It is the degree of learning necessary to perform coordinated skills which primarily serves to differentiate them from the more gross bodily movements placed in the first classification.

2.10 Hand-Finger Movements

Behaviors in this class are characterized by the sense of touch rather than the sense of sight. The use of Braille by the visually-handicapped is a primary example of this class of behavior.

To be able to translate a paragraph in Braille accurately.

To be able to differentiate between a quarter and a nickel solely by touch.

2.20 Hand-Eye Coordination

Objectives related to this classification emphasize hand-eye relationships. Activities involving hand-eye coordination are extremely numerous. Several of the most common are playing a musical instrument, typing, writing, sewing, painting, sculpting, and weaving. Note that in all of these behaviors the feedback provided from visual inspection is critical to the successful performance of the task.

To be able to type an average of 60 words per minute for five minutes with fewer than four errors.

To be able to paint a portrait of a woman in the cubistic mode.

To be able to print the letters of the alphabet, duplicating the model in the writing manual.

2.30 Hand-Ear Coordination

Behaviors in this area focus on the relationships between sound stimuli and hand or finger movements. The sound in this case may serve as a stimulus for the hand movement or as a source of feedback concerning the success of the movement pattern. Examples of activities involving hand-ear coordination are found primarily in applied music (not involving sight-reading music), the broadcast media, and some other performing arts.

To be able to move the microphone lever to the right within two seconds after the music stops.

Given a note played on the violin, to be able to find the same note on the piano.

2.40 Hand-Eye-Foot Coordination

Objectives in this classification relate to movements which involve coordinated movements by hands, feet, arms, and fingers in conjunction with the eye. Most objectives in this area relate to such activities as physical education and operation of technical equipment and machinery.

To be able to punt a football 20 yards.
To be able to operate a sheet metal lathe safely.

2.50 Other Combinations of Hand-Foot-Eye-Ear Movements

This classification of objectives includes more complex behaviors that involve coordinated movements other than those specified in classes 2.10 through 2.40. Activities which might be included in this classification include piano tuning (eye-ear-hand), playing such musical instruments as organ, harp, and trap drums (eye-ear-hand-foot), and driving a car (eye-ear-hand-foot).

To be able to tune a piano through the use of a tuning fork.
To be able to drive a car along a prescribed route for three blocks without violating any traffic laws.
To be able to sight-read and play a given piece of organ music with no more than three mistakes.

3.00 NON-VERBAL COMMUNICATION BEHAVIORS

Objectives relating to nonverbal communication behaviors are frequently found in public speaking, theatre, dance, and related performing arts curricula. The nonverbal communication behaviors included in this section (1) are learned and (2) attempt to convey a message to a receiver without the use of words. Some nonverbal behaviors serve to complement verbal communication. For purposes of clarification, those objectives will be classified under Category 4.00 as an integral part of speech communication. Nonverbal communication behaviors in this section include facial expressions, gestures, bodily movements or a combination of the three.

3.10 Facial Expression

This classification focuses primarily on the mouth and eyes as communicators of moods or messages. Objectives involving facial expressions are especially important in theatre.

To be able to portray the emotion "rage" via facial expressions.

To be able to exhibit a range of six facial expressions which communicate different emotions identifiable by a panel of observers.

3.20 Gestures

Objectives in this class of behaviors involve the use of hands and arms to communicate specific messages. Areas in which gestures are primary forms of communication range from the complex language of the deaf to some forms of dances (for example, the hula), to the gesture of the thumb used by the hitchhiker. Most objectives related to the use of gestures are found in public speaking, theatre, and dance curricula.

To be able to communicate accurately a given message in hand-sign language.

To be able to communicate a series of five messages solely by the use of gestures so they may be understood by a panel of observers.

3.20 Bodily Movement

Objectives in this classification relate to total bodily movements whose primary emphases are the communication of a message or series of messages. Frequently, facial expressions and gestures are incorporated into a total pattern of movement. The defining characteristic of this class of behaviors is the movement of the trunk in addition to the other limbs in an attempt to communicate a message. Pantomimes are the most common activity which incorporate entire patterns of bodily movement.

To be able to portray, without words, a lady golfer hitting a hole-in-one.

To be able to pantomime a message selected at random so that a panel of observers can verbalize the message accurately.

4.00 SPEECH BEHAVIORS

Objectives related to speech behaviors primarily are found in speech communication, public speaking, and speech correction curricula.

The communication cycle may be subdivided into component processess – message invention, organization, encoding, transmission, reception, decoding, evaluation, and response. Some of these processes are primarily cognitive and affective, while others may be classified more readily in the psychomotor domain. Objectives related to message invention, organization, encoding, decoding, and evaluation are classified under Levels five and six (Synthesis and Evaluation) of the cognitive domain. Most objectives related to these processes would be classified under Section 5.10 (Production of a Unique Communication).

Message reception and response would be classified under Levels one and two of the affective domain (Receiving and Responding). Consequently, the only phase of the speech communication process related to this classification is transmission. This involves the formation, production, and projection of sound.

Gestures and other physical movements which tend to complement or reinforce verbal messages also are classified in this section. Those gestures and physical movements which are designed to replace or substitute for verbal messages are classified in Section 3.00.

4.10 Sound Production

Objectives in this classification relate to the ability to produce *meaningful* sounds. This involves the processes of respiration and phonation or the forcing of air past the vocal folds in such a way as to produce an audible sound which is designed to communicate to a listener. Random babbling of infants is not considered to be meaningful sound production.

To be able to produce the vowel sounds.

Given a series of sounds on a tape recorder, to be able to imitate them vocally.

4.20 Sound-Word Formation

This involves the ability to coordinate sounds into meaningful words and messages. The processes involved in word formation include articulation and modification of the oral cavity to form a battery of different sounds.

To be able to say the words "red" and "read" so that their meaning may be distinguished by a group of non-expert listeners.

To be able to recite a given passage without mispronouncing any words.

4.30 Sound Projection

Objectives in this classification involve the ability to project sounds across the air waves at a level adequate for reception and decoding by the listener. The processes of respiration and modification of the resonators are involved primarily in sound projection.

To be able to say a given word in a soundproof chamber at a level of 15 decibels.

Given a room filled with people generating a noise level of 20 decibels, to be able to convey an oral message to another person across the room 25 feet away with 95 percent comprehension.

4.40 Sound-Gesture Coordination

This classification deals with the ability to coordinate facial expression, movement, and gestures with verbal messages. The goal of nonverbal and verbal coordination is the enhancement of the verbal message through the nonverbal channels. Objectives which involve total nonverbal communication are placed in Section 3.00.

Given a verbal message three minutes in length, to be able to transmit the same message with no significant reduction in comprehension in half the time through the addition of coordinated gestures and bodily movement to the verbal message.

Given an ambiguous verbal message, to be able to transmit the intended meaning accurately to your classmates through the addition of meaningful facial expressions.

SUMMARY

The authors of the present text believe that the taxonomies can be valuable educational tools but that they are not appropriate to all objectives, especially those involving complex behaviors. The above discussion of the three behavioral domains is intended as a guide for the classification of behavioral objectives. It should not be regarded as an absolute answer to the problems associated with classifying educational objectives and human behavior.

CHAPTER IV

Writing Informational Objectives

You will recall that a distinction was made in Chapter I between behavioral objectives for planning and evaluating instruction and behavioral objectives for informing others of what you hope to accomplish in an instructional unit. The purpose of this chapter is to teach you how to write instructional objectives in behavioral terms for the purpose of communicating your instructional intent to other teachers, administrators, students, and anyone else who wants to know what you plan to teach.

The informational objective you will learn about here is a much less specific and less detailed objective than the planning objectives discussed in Chapter II, but they have considerable value in education.

1. Administrators and curriculum planners use them as a basis for their curriculum decisions.
2. They are included in the college catalogues that advisors and students read to decide whether or not to take a course.
3. They are included in a course syllabus and frequently have a profound effect on how students perform in a course.
4. Registrars read them to determine whether course credit can be transferred from one institution to another.
5. Teachers use them to evaluate the quality of instructional content.

You should recall from Chapters I and II that the major characteristic of the informational objective is that it names the observable behavior that the student will exhibit when demonstrating mastery of a particular unit of instruction. Action terms such as *write, compute, identify, list*, and *describe orally* are used since they refer to observable behavior, and terms such as *to know, to understand*, or *to appreciate* are avoided since they do not refer to observable behavior. In addition to describing the behavior to be expected, the major characteristics of the product the student is to produce should be specified.

The greater the clarity with which these two elements are specified, the greater the probability that an objective will communicate clearly what is to be learned from a unit of instruction. However, it should be pointed out that objectives need not always specify these two elements in minute detail. The important thing is that from what the objective states, a person is able to infer the kind of behavior and the kind of product that is desired. In other words, if most people who read an objective can agree independently as to what these two elements are, then the objective can be considered acceptable. Similarly, if several people independently can produce similar test items to evaluate the achievement of an objective, it indicates that the objective is unambiguous.

Thus, all you need to do to write instructional objectives which clearly communicate is to write objectives which specify these two elements (*i.e.*, the observable behavior and the product mentioned). Now if you would like to have a little practice in discriminating between acceptable informational objectives and nonacceptable informational objectives – and in writing informational objectives for the cognitive domain of behaviors – you will want to complete the material which follows. If, on the other hand, you only wanted to know what an informational objective consists of, then you have just completed this chapter.

PROGRAMED PRACTICE IN IDENTIFYING AND WRITING INFORMATIONAL OBJECTIVES*

Read the following objective:

After completing this lesson, the student will be able to write the name of 10 of the last 15 presidents of the United States.

The two elements of an informational objective in this objective are:

behavior

"After completing this lesson, the student will be able to write the

product

names of 10 of the last 15 presidents of the United States."

Now read the next objective and underline and label the two elements of an informational objective.

At the end of the course, the student will be able to write a short essay demonstrating proper use of eight major punctuation marks.

Now turn the page and check your answers.

*When there is a question in the programed practice which follows regarding whether a word or phrase should be underlined as a behavior or product or not underlined because it is a condition of learning, underline the behavioral or product element as completely as possible in each sentence. See the answer on page 82 for an example of this condition.

Answer

behavior

At the end of the course the student will be able to write a short essay

product

demonstrating proper use of the eight major punctuation marks.

Identify the two elements in the following objective:

Students will be able to draw proportionally accurate drawings of one-celled organisms from observing them in a microscope.

Now turn the page and check your answers.

Answer

behavior product

Students will be able to draw proportionally accurate drawings

product behavior

of one-celled organisms from observing them in a microscope.

Identify the two elements in the following objective.

The student will give a speech to a live audience that is designed to persuade the members to change their attitude toward something. The major persuasive techniques taught in the course must be applied in the speech.

Now turn the page and check your answers.

Answer

behavior

The student will give a speech to a live audience that is designed to persuade the members to change their attitude toward something. The major persuasive techniques taught in the course must be applied in the speech.

product

Read the following objectives and underline the behavioral and product elements that are present in each objective. One or more elements may be absent. Use a dashed line when underlining the behavioral element and an unbroken line when underlining the product element.

1. Students will be able to describe in writing how principles of civil rights apply to current events.
2. Students will be able to state orally the correct time for any clock settings.
3. The student will learn the names of six common tools in metal shop.
4. The student will understand how paper is made.
5. The student will learn to write properly.
6. Students will be able to identify in writing the political orientation of various newspapers from reading several editorials from each newspaper.

Now turn to the next page and check yourself.

Answer

1. Students will be able to describe in writing how principles of civil rights apply to current events.
2. Students will be able to state orally the correct time for any clock settings.
3. The student will learn the names of six common tools in metal shop.
4. The student will understand how paper is made.
5. The student will learn to write properly.
6. Students will be able to identify in writing the political orientation of various newspapers from reading several editorials from each newspaper.

Below are two non-informational objectives. Rewrite them so that they specify a behavior and a product.

1. At the end of the course the student will understand the fundamental concepts of long division.

_____

_____

_____

_____

2. The student will learn about the structure and organization of Congress.

_____

_____

_____

_____

Underline the behavior and the product in each of your restated objectives. If both are present, your objectives are probably acceptable. Now turn to the next page and look at our restated objectives.

There are several ways to state these two objectives behaviorally, and one is no more correct than another. It is only important that some form of behavior and some type of product are prescribed. Following are a few variations of each objective.

1. The student will be able to solve long division problems.

1. The student will describe in writing the steps involved in solving long division problems.

1. The student will list the arithmetic operations required for solving long division problems.

1. The student will be able to identify long division problems which have been worked properly and problems which are incorrectly worked.

2. The student will draw an organizational diagram of Congress, showing the units and relationships between units.

2. The student will be able to write an essay describing the structure and organization of Congress.

2. The student will select from organizational descriptions the one which accurately describes the organization of Congress.

Restate the following two objectives so that they are informational.

1. The course will deal with the major trends in painting in the nineteenth century.

_____

_____

_____

_____

2. Students will develop a clear understanding of the biological principle of photosynthesis.

_____

_____

_____

_____

Underline the behavior and the product in each of your objectives to make sure they are clearly specified and then look at our interpretations.

1. Students will be able to write a description of the major trends in painting in the nineteenth century.
1. Students will name the major painters of the nineteenth century and describe their principle works.
2. The student will describe the process of photosynthesis orally.
2. Students will be able to draw a diagram with labels showing the principle of photosynthesis.

By this time you should be able to write informational objectives which clearly communicate what you want students to be able to do after completing instruction. Before we go on to the final section in this chapter, write three informational objectives just to demonstrate your newly acquired skill. You might wish to write them for a course you have had or one you are taking now, or you may wish to write them for a course you are teaching or are planning to teach. Remember to include both elements.

1. _____

_____

_____

_____

2. _____

_____

_____

_____

3. _____

_____

_____

_____

Hopefully, it is not necessary to underline the behavior and product on these three objectives.

WRITING INFORMATIONAL OBJECTIVES FOR THE COGNITIVE DOMAIN*

In writing objectives for various categories of the *Taxonomy of Educational Objectives: Cognitive Domain* (Bloom, *et al.* 1956), a major difficulty is frequently encountered: many behavioral objectives can be classified legitimately into more than one category. For example, an objective such as this:

> The student will be able to write a paper describing the major causes of the Civil War.

could be categorized in the knowledge, comprehension, application, analysis, and synthesis categories. If the student learned the three major causes of the Civil War from reading the text and merely is expected to recall what he read, then it is a *knowledge* objective. If the student learned the information in the course and he is expected to translate the information into his own terms in the paper, it is *comprehension*. If the student learned a procedure for identifying the cause of wars during the course but did not deal with the Civil War, then applying this procedure to the Civil War would be an example of *application*. Writing a description of the causes of the Civil War could be the end product of *analysis* or *synthesis*, providing the student previously had not analyzed or synthesized information dealing with the causes of the Civil War.

From this illustration you should be convinced that problems in writing objectives which can be categorized into only one taxonomic category do exist. You also might have picked up a clue from the illustration as to how this problem can be solved. The solution to the problem is to include a statement in your objective which specifies the type of experience (including the lack of experience) the student has had with the subject matter prior to demonstrating achievement of the objective. The objective also should indicate how he is to deal with the subject matter in demonstrating mastery performance; that is, whether he is to break down information (analysis), put information together (synthesis), translate it

*Interested students will find the system developed by Metfessel, Michael, and Kirsner (1969) useful for writing behavioral objectives for the cognitive and affective domains. A copy of their system is contained in Appendix C.

from one form to another (comprehension), recall or recognize information (knowledge), apply a known procedure to a new situation (application), or evaluate something according to some criterion (evaluation).

Knowledge objectives require students to reproduce or recall something that they have experienced previously, in the same or similar form. Adding a phrase such as the one below to the previous objective clearly should limit the objective to the knowledge category.

> The student will be able to write a paper describing the major causes of the Civil War. The description should resemble closely the information presented during the course.

Comprehension objectives require students to reproduce or recall something previously experienced in a *new* form. An added phrase such as the one that follows should restrict the objective to the comprehension category.

> The description will be a translation from the information presented in the textbook to the student's own words.

Application objectives require students to use previously experienced procedures or knowledge in *new* situations. However, so do analysis, synthesis, and evaluation objectives. Thus, care must be taken to make it clear which type of performance is intended. A phrase like the following should identify the objective as application.

> The knowledge of factors causing other wars discussed in the course should be applied in writing the paper.

Analysis objectives require students to break down into its component elements something which they have not broken down previously. The following phrase would identify the objective as belonging to the analysis category.

> The student will analyze – and base his paper upon his analysis – a description of the major events and relevant conditions existing prior to the War.

Synthesis objectives require students to put something together which they have not put together previously. To make the example objective a synthesis objective, make the following addition.

> The paper should be the student's original interpretation of the War's causes.

Evaluation objectives require students to render judgments regarding something for which they have not rendered judgments previously. The example objective would have to be entirely rewritten for this category.

> The student will be able to evaluate various interpretations of the causes of the Civil War by applying evaluative criteria which were employed in the course for evaluating interpretations of other wars.

To review the guidelines just presented, identify the appropriate taxonomic category for each of the objectives below. Write the category names in the blanks provided.

1. _____: The student will be able to write an essay employing the three types of paragraph organization given in class.
2. _____: Given the names of several composers and the names of several symphonies covered in class, the student will be able to match them correctly on a test.
3. _____: The student will be able to identify the major parts of speech in several unfamiliar sentences.
4. _____: The student will identify the major positive and negative features of unfamiliar political systems according to the criteria presented in class.
5. _____: Given unfamiliar statistical data in paragraph form, the student will be able to present the information in graphic form.
6. _____: The student will be able to design a building according to unfamiliar specifications and restrictions.

Check your answers on the next page.

Answers:

1. Application
2. Knowledge
3. Analysis
4. Evaluation
5. Comprehension
6. Synthesis

We hope you agreed with us on most of them.

For practice that is closer to actually writing objectives, rewrite the following objective to fit into each of the taxonomic categories. Make sure the objective fits in only one category.

The student will be able to list the major effects of industrialization on the American culture.

Knowledge: _____

_____

_____

_____

_____

Comprehension: _____

_____

_____

_____

_____

Application: _____

_____

Analysis:

Synthesis:

Evaluation:

To check yourself, read your new objectives and make sure the kind of experience the student was to have with the subject matter prior to demonstrating achievement of the objective is implied clearly and conforms to the guidelines specified on pages 93 and 94.

As a result of completing this section, you should now be able to:

1. Define an informational objective.
2. Identify the behavioral and product elements in an informational objective.
3. Translate nonacceptable informational objectives into acceptable informational objectives.
4. Write objectives for specific categories in the cognitive domain.

For further examples of objectives in the cognitive domain, see Chapter 3 and Appendix A. Unfortunately, all of the objectives in these locations do not contain the necessary elements for informational objectives, nor do they contain the necessary information for discrete classification in taxonomic categories. But since you have already learned the proper way to state informational objectives, you should not learn improper habits from examining them.

WRITING INFORMATIVE OBJECTIVES FOR THE AFFECTIVE DOMAIN*

Writing objectives for the affective domain is quite different from writing objectives for the cognitive domain, primarily because of the difficulty in observing and measuring people's interests, attitudes, and values. Interests, attitudes, and values are essentially generalizations about the things people do. A person who reads a great deal on his own can be described as being interested in reading. A person who consistently chooses to watch football games on TV in preference to listening to symphonies can be described as liking football more than symphonies. A person who votes in all elections, participates in civic affairs, keeps abreast of local and national developments, and doesn't break laws might be described as "a good citizen" or one might say that he "believes in" the

*A useful system for writing objectives for both the cognitive and affective domains appears in Appendix C. This system was developed by Metfessel, Michael and Kirsner (1969).

way in which our government works. A person who eats wholesome food, exercises daily, gets plenty of sleep, brushes his teeth three times a day, and gets a physical check-up twice a year can be said to value his health. A person who listens mostly to popular radio music and buys mostly popular records can be said to prefer popular music to other types of music. A person who continually does things for another person, arranges to be with the other person, and expresses affection both verbally and physically toward the person can be said to like or even love that person. But it is obviously impossible to expect teachers to assess actual attitudinal behaviors such as these. Thus, we are faced with two alternatives: we can give up the idea of trying to observe and measure attitudes altogether, or we can resort to asking students to tell us what they do under various circumstances and to describe their interests and preferences. The latter alternative, although frought with flaws and inadequacies, is what is recommended. The reason we choose this alternative is that if no attempts are made to measure attitudinal changes, attitudinal objectives may tend to be more and more de-emphasized, if not forgotten.

Given that we are stuck with observing attitudes in the form of student reports of their past behavior, predictions of their future behavior, and statements of beliefs and preferences, what is the best way to do it? One way would be to question students orally in either a formal or informal situation. Perhaps the major disadvantage of this procedure is that the teacher's presence may have a very strong influence on students' responses. They may say things that they know the teacher wants to hear, and the teacher may inadvertantly cause students to respond in various ways by the way he states the questions and the way he reacts to students' responses.

The other approach to measuring attitudes is to use a paper-pencil questionnaire. This is probably the most typical method employed in assessing attitudes. The problem of students responding in a "socially desirable" way rather than the way they really feel still exists with the questionnaire, but that response may be less than in a face-to-face interview situation.

In using either method it is highly recommended that students be informed clearly that there will be *no* consequences to their responses (*i.e.*, they will not be graded, their academic program will not be modified, etc.) and that their responses are to be used to evaluate the effects of the instructional program – not to evaluate them.

The first of two major types of attitudinal responses requested on paper-pencil instruments are items requesting the student to report how often he engages in various activities, for example, "How often have you visited our art museum in the past year?" or "How many novels have you read of your own volition in the past month?"

The second type of items are those that request the student to report his feelings, opinions, preferences, or values on some topic. For example, "Do you enjoy learning about history?" "What is your favorite school subject?" "Do you think people should smoke?" Questionnaire items can be made in various forms, of which the following five are exemplary:

1. *Yes - No:*

   Do you enjoy looking at buildings and structures? Yes ☐ No ☐

2. *Scaled:*

   How often do you initiate conversation with others about national affairs?

   Never ☐ Sometimes ☐ Always ☐

   To what extent do you obey the playground regulations?

   not at all ☐ ☐ ☐ ☐ ☐ to a great extent

3. *Rank order:*

   Rank the following leisure time activities in order of your preference:

   Swimming____ Reading____ TV watching____ etc.

4. *Multiple choice:*

   Which would you rather do during a one-hour free choice period at school:

   _____a. read stories

   _____b. make an art mural for the hall

   _____c. have group singing

5. *Open ended:*
Briefly describe your feelings about the equality of people. _____

_____

_____

What should be done about stating attitudinal objectives? The most honest approach is to state your objectives in terms of the actual behavior you intend to observe. For example, "Students will indicate on a questionnaire at the end of the course that they like studying biology much more now than they did prior to beginning the course."

The other approach is to state your objectives in non-measurable terms, such as "Students will like studying biology much more after the course than before," or "Students will increase their enjoyment of classical music," or "Students will read articles on current affairs more often after completing the course than they did prior to taking the course." You are invited to choose whichever method you prefer.

For further information on the affective domain, you are referred to the second section of Chapter III and also to Appendix A, where several example objectives are presented. Robert Mager's (1968) *Developing Attitude Toward Learning* also should be helpful when specifying attitudinal objectives and designing procedures for achieving them.

WRITING INFORMATIONAL OBJECTIVES FOR THE PSYCHOMOTOR DOMAIN

The psychomotor domain is by far the easiest domain for which to write objectives. The primary reason for this is that the behaviors in the psychomotor domain generally are observable clearly and almost always objectively measureable. For this reason, instruction and practice in writing psychomotor objectives will not be provided. Instead, the reader is referred to the third section of Chapter III and Appendix A, where several examples of psychomotor objectives are provided.

CHAPTER V

The Influence of Behavioral Objectives in Education

The first section of this chapter covers the implications of using behavioral objectives at various educational grade levels. The second section discusses how these objectives may be used by various participants involved in the educational process. The third section examines the influence of the school environment on the objectives.

APPLICATION OF BEHAVIORAL OBJECTIVES TO SPECIFIED EDUCATIONAL LEVELS

Discussions in previous chapters may have given some readers the impression that a behavioral objective for one educational level is not much different from an objective for another educational level. It is time to clear up any such misconceptions.

Personal experience and developmental research suggest that individuals acquire capacities to perform different skills and intellectual operations at various periods during development. (McCandless, 1967; McDonald, 1965; Bloom, 1964; DeCecco, 1968). Behavior patterns for a given individual vary in rate of development and may vary substantially from individual to individual (Edwards and Scannell, 1968). Moreover, students of learning also may recall that there are a variety of types of learning, that these different types of learning may be sequential, and that a given type of learning may be contingent upon previously learned behaviors (Gagné, 1965a; Gagné, 1965b; and Glaser, 1962).

Obviously, the extent and kind of information to be acquired, applied, analyzed, synthesized, and evaluated differ between preschool and graduate programs. The specific psychomotor skills and attitudes to be acquired also vary as a function of educational level.

Behavioral objectives must be viewed in light of many different variables in the educational setting. Perhaps one of the more critical variables which affects their use is the level of education for which objectives are intended. Several important distinctions among objectives at differing educational levels should be pointed out.

Figure 3 emphasizes a *general tendency*: as the educational level increases, the complexity of behaviors (and objectives) required increases. But the relationship suggested in Figure 3 is just a tendency. We do not intend to imply a one-to-one relationship regarding educational level and task complexity. Anyone who has taught in an elementary classroom knows that small children are capable of performing some very complex tasks. However, the child in the first grade more likely will be given objectives which emphasize the acquisition of basic skills frequently implemented through drill and practice, while students in higher education

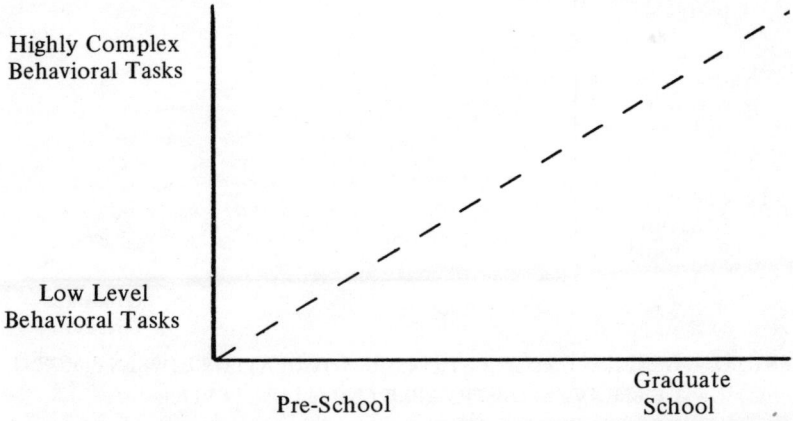

FIGURE 3. GENERALIZED RELATIONSHIP SPECULATED BETWEEN GRADE LEVELS AND COMPLEXITY OF TASKS REQUIRED.

situations frequently will be given objectives that emphasize applying, organizing, problem solving, and other concept manipulation tasks. The point is, it frequently becomes more difficult to formulate objectives and measure the outcomes of instruction as the educational level increases.

The relationship between grade level and observable behaviors is exceedingly complex and cannot be expressed completely in a simple graph. It is possible to express a *general tendency* for the two to be related, and we have done this in Figure 4. Again, a *tendency* is being expressed in Figure 4; there is no intention to imply a one-to-one relationship. Figure 4 emphasizes that the behaviors desired at lower educational levels frequently are observable (*e.g.*, psychomotor behaviors), while behaviors desired at higher levels tend to be less observable (often affective and cognitive behaviors).* An objective for a child of kindergarten age such as "place the square block in the square hole" involves considerably less complex skills than an objective for a post-doctoral seminar such as "given the desired characteristics of a proposed synthetic plastic, develop a material which meets the desired specifications and provide a projected cost analysis for full-scale production."

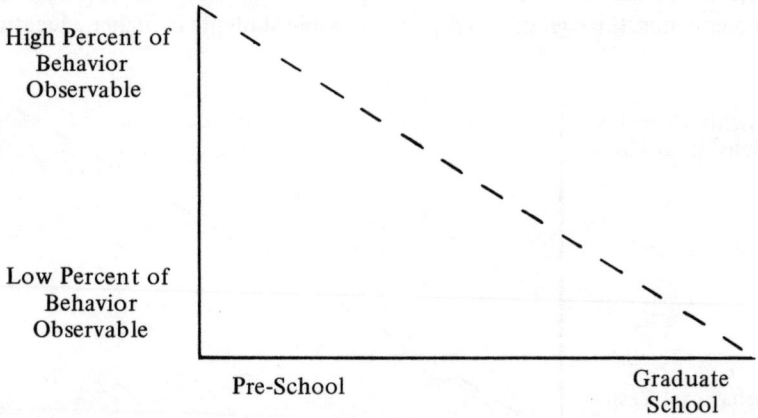

FIGURE 4. GENERALIZED RELATIONSHIP SPECULATED BETWEEN PERCENT OF BEHAVIOR OBSERVABLE AND GRADE LEVELS.

*This observation was first suggested to one of the authors by William R. McKenzie of Southern Illinois University in a doctoral seminar in 1966.

It follows from the above contentions that the learner increases (or should increase) his responsibility for learning quite rapidly as educational levels increase. Increasing the complexity and decreasing the observable behaviors as a function of educational level suggest the learner has little option but to become a more independent learner.

The higher the level of instruction the more ambiguous and difficult to measure are the objectives. Many objectives at higher levels involve learning outside the context of the classroom. The result is that the observable behaviors are reduced for product evaluation. At lower levels most learning of desired skills occurs in class under the observation of the teacher. The measurement of these skills is made easier and more complete. Ideally, as the level of education increases, the relationship between planning objectives and competencies required for real-life tasks also increases.

Realizing that such differences occur when using objectives at different instructional levels, teachers and administrators should attempt to adapt the specificity level and measurement level of objectives to appropriate grade levels, or better still, to the levels of individual students. Moreover, planning objectives that are based on real-life competencies should be specified as soon and as frequently as possible. Measurement of objectives should be attempted at all levels regardless of the complexity of the objective or the ambiguity of the task desired. Successful measurement is not only dependent on level of instruction but on the creativity of the instructional planner and objective developer.

Some of the early work of Bobbitt (1918, 1924), Charters (1923, 1929), and Charters and Waples (1929), in which systematic procedures were employed to formulate detailed objectives for education, provide some indication of the complexity gradient at various grade levels.

THE RELATIONSHIP OF BEHAVIORAL OBJECTIVES TO PARTICIPANTS IN THE EDUCATIONAL PROCESS

The philosophy underlying the use of behavioral objectives has already been discussed in a previous chapter. The purpose of this section is to illustrate how the philosophy applies to those persons directly or indirectly involved with the educational process. Behavioral objectives serve all who are involved in the teaching-learning process, particularly students, teachers, administrators, school boards, and parents.

BEHAVIORAL OBJECTIVES AND STUDENTS

Research concerned with the transfer of learning indicates that students generally do not apply learned skills or knowledge to practical situations unless the teacher specifically demonstrates the application. The popular phrase in academic circles which reflects this body of research is "teach for transfer." The teacher attempting to implement this strategy makes desired behaviors explicit and specifies the variety of conditions under which the behaviors or skills may be applied after they have been adequately learned. When behavioral objectives are given directly to students, the exact behaviors desired and the conditions under which the behaviors are to be exhibited are specified. By being given behavioral objectives, students do not have to guess what is expected of them in the learning setting. Learners may spend their time acquiring behaviors specified by the teacher rather than attempting to infer what the teacher expects of them.

Some recent research has demonstrated that when students are given a list of specific behavioral objectives for a course, they tend to perform better on objective examinations than when they are not aware of specific course objectives (Miles, Kibler and Pettigrew, 1967). It stands to reason that if students know what is expected of them, they will expend less random energy studying unimportant material and concentrate on learning important skills.

One final value of giving behavioral objectives to students is intangible yet very important. It is the sense of security a student experiences when he knows what specifically is expected from him in a course and the conditions under which he will be expected to exhibit his competencies. Psychologists suggest that generalized fears cause greater emotional anxiety than specific well-defined fears. Behavioral objectives can help students understand specific requirements of a course and also reduce the amount of generalized anxiety about course requirements.

BEHAVIORAL OBJECTIVES AND TEACHERS*

The value of behavioral objectives to the teacher is dependent, of course, upon the level of instruction, the subject matter of the course, the

*Teachers interested in an opportunity to share their behavioral objectives with other teachers and to obtain copies of objectives used by other teachers will want to read Appendix D, which briefly explains a program to encourage the exchange of behavioral objectives.

nature of school system, and countless other variables related to the instructional environment. However, there appear to be at least two values of objectives (for teachers) which remain constant in most teaching situations. First, objectives prompt teachers to determine the most significant aspect of subject matter to be learned. At the college level, students often joke that a specific course (*e.g.*, Advanced Theories of Learning) is, in reality, a course in Professor X. In other words, the professor makes no attempt to define critical elements of subject matter related to the course but only talks about theories of learning of interest to him. In rare situations a course in Professor X may be desirable and useful, but from a curriculum viewpoint such a course creates a void of information in a student's educational background which might be important in the future. If teachers discipline themselves to analyze the content of specific courses for which they are responsible, the problem of majoring on minors or dwelling on unimportant issues will become less critical. It should be emphasized at this point that this value of objectives is not held universally by all educators.

A second value of objectives to teachers is their aid in establishing criteria for the measurement of classroom achievement. Most teachers have had the experience of teaching a unit in a course and then spending long torturous hours attempting to devise ways of measuring what the students have learned. Teachers often find that had they approached the subject matter in a slightly different manner or modified instructional strategies, the measure of classroom achievement could have been greatly simplified and improved (*i.e.*, made more reliable and valid). Behavioral objectives require teachers to specify criteria for acceptable behaviors and determine in advance how acceptable performance will be measured. Thus measurement in the classroom may be improved.

A side effect of these two values for teachers is similar to that experienced by students. The teacher who is confident (1) that the subject matter being presented is of prime importance and (2) that measurement of achievement is efficient and appropriate to course goals, is more secure in his position and, consequently, is usually more satisfied with his professional contribution.

BEHAVIORAL OBJECTIVES AND ADMINISTRATORS

Behavioral objectives are important at two levels of administration. The administrator responsible for designing and coordinating curricula (in conjunction with the instructional staff) relies on behavioral objectives to insure that content and subject matter are covered adequately and that there are minimal overlaps between courses, especially within related areas. The use of behavioral objectives also promotes consistency and a thread of continuity among related courses. Continuity is especially important in a series of courses where there is an introductory section followed by an intermediate or advanced section.

When the administrator is supervisor and teacher-evaluator, behavioral objectives help him in a different way. The objectives (1) suggest the degree of progress desired at a point in the course in light of the predetermined sequence of units and (2) help determine if teachers are pursuing adequately the goals of the course. When the behavioral objectives are developed by the teacher, they give the supervising administrator insight into the teacher's philosophy and course goals. This freedom to develop individual objectives is more prevalent at higher levels of instruction.

BEHAVIORAL OBJECTIVES AND SCHOOL BOARDS

One of the persistent problems in education is to obtain adequate funds for the maintenance of a quality educational program. *School board* refers to the group of citizens who control funds in an educational setting. In the college context the term *board of trustees* or perhaps the *committee on education* would be substituted for the term *school board.*

In order to defend an existing budget or demonstrate the need for increased funds, administrators and teachers often are required to describe the existing educational program or some proposed addition to the curriculum. It is difficult to provide the board with a verbal or verbal-pictorial representation of the learning situation as it really exists, because board members are often far removed from the classroom. However, when a school system requires behavioral objectives for courses, it is possible to demonstrate the content of courses in objective form to a school board and thus demonstrate, more concretely than might otherwise be possible, precisely what learning achievements occur in a given classroom on a given day. This concrete representation of the educational program often may have some communicative or persuasive value to a school board. Thus, behavioral objectives may help educate and persuade those persons in charge of educational funds.

BEHAVIORAL OBJECTIVES AND PARENTS

The parent is often neglected as a participant in the educational process. However, parents are becoming increasingly concerned about the quality of education in the school and are, therefore, becoming more involved with their children's educational growth and classroom problems. When students are given behavioral objectives, the parents may also elect to study them and determine what behaviors are expected of their child during the school year. Although we are unaware of the existence of such a practice, we feel that a procedure of periodically sending home a list of the actual objectives achieved by a student would be a marked improvement over the grade report card procedure commonly used. Parents could, thereby, gauge the progress of their child at intervals during the year to help insure that proper levels of achievement are being maintained. It is, of course, desirable that parents confer with teachers as well as with their children about educational achievement, but the presence of behavioral objectives can serve to make parents more familiar with the child's desired growth and, in some instances, indicate areas where the child needs special help outside of the classroom.

Parents may be overly concerned about minor points in the curriculum which were stressed when they were in school. The specification of *major* objectives can help parents emphasize and reinforce the goals being sought by the teacher and can alleviate tendencies on the part of some parents to stress relatively unimportant concepts to their children.

THE ENVIRONMENT OF THE SCHOOL AND THE USE OF BEHAVIORAL OBJECTIVES

The educational environment in a classroom or within departments of a university can influence profoundly the value and use of behavioral objectives. In the homogeneous classroom or in the college class primarily composed of majors in a given discipline, the objectives will probably be more valuable and realistic in light of the criteria specified for measuring desired achievement. When heterogeneous classes exist and when college courses include students with a variety of interests and major areas of study, the specification of performance criteria is often unrealistic for students at extreme ends of the achievement continuum. Therefore, the objectives should be flexible when possible and primarily serve as a guide rather than as a straight-jacket for the teacher. The teacher should analyze the socioeconomic and educational structure of students in a class and determine whether or not a set of rigid behavioral objectives would be desirable and useful. This reemphasizes a point which has been made earlier – that objectives must be tailored to individual needs. A set of blanket objectives could do more harm than good in some classes or types of educational programs.

A second environmental variable which relates to the success of the behavioral objective is the attitude of the school system toward educational innovations. In a school system that encourages creative education, the objectives can serve to standardize content matter across modes of instruction, insuring that subject matter is not omitted or distorted as a result of the new teaching strategy. Behavioral objectives appear to be more valuable in an educational environment where creativity and innovation is encouraged. Behavioral objectives are also useful in an educational system which is static, but their value there is in curriculum standardization rather than in maintaining consistency across a wide variety of instructional strategies.

A school system's standards also affects the use of behavioral objectives. When academic standards are emphasized and measured, objectives can provide assessments of educational progress and eliminate much subjectivity and guesswork in evaluation of teachers' and students' performance. In systems that have relaxed standards and do not attempt to evaluate teachers or students, objectives have less value.

In conclusion, the educational environment plays an important role in determining whether objectives can be profitable, desirable, and useful. Objectives must be geared to a given teacher and class in the context of a particular school system in order to be of maximum value.

Bibliography

Ammerman, H. L., & Melching, W. H. (1966), *The derivation, analysis, and classification of instructional objectives.* Alexandria, Virginia: George Washington University.

Bloom, B. S. (1964), *Stability and change in human characteristics.* New York: John Wiley & Sons.

Bloom, B. S. (1968), Learning for mastery. *Evaluation Comment,* **1** (2).

Bloom, B. S. (Ed.) Engelhart, M. D., Furst, E. J., Hill, W. H., & Krathwohl, D. R. (1956), *Taxonomy of educational objectives – the classification of educational goals, Handbook I: cognitive domain.* New York: David McKay Company, Inc.

Bobbitt, F. (1918), *The curriculum.* Boston: Houghton-Mifflin.

Bobbitt, F. (1924), *How to make a curriculum.* Boston: Houghton-Mifflin.

Cardinal principles of secondary education (1937). Bulletin No. 35. Washington, D. C.: United States Government Printing Office.

Carroll, J. (1963), A model of school learning. *Teachers College Record,* **64**, 723-733.

Charters, W. W. (1923), *Curriculum construction.* New York: Macmillan.

Charters, W. W. (1929), *The teaching of ideals.* New York: Macmillan.

Charters, W. W., & Waples, D. (1929), *The commonwealth teacher-training study.* Chicago: Univers. of Chicago Press.

Chenzoff, A. P., & Folley, J. D., Jr. (July, 1965), *Guidelines for training situation and analysis.* Technical Report NAVTRADEVCEN 1218-4, Contract Number N 61339-1218. Valencia, Pennsylvania: Applied Science Associates, Inc.

Congreve, W. J. (1965), Independent learning. *North Central Association Quarterly*, **40**, 222-228.

DeCecco, J. P. (1968), *The psychology of learning and instruction: educational psychology*. Englewood Cliffs, New Jersey: Prentice-Hall.

Ebel, R. L. (1965), *Measuring education achievement*. Englewood Cliffs, New Jersey: Prentice-Hall.

Educational Policies Commission (1961), *The central purposes of american education*, Washington, D. C.: Educational Policies Commission of the National Education Association.

Edwards, A. J., & Scannell, D. P. (1968), *Educational psychology: the teaching-learning process*. Scranton, Pennsylvania: International Textbook.

English, H. B., & English, A. C. (1958), *A comprehensive dictionary of psychological and psychoanalytical terms*. New York: David McKay.

French, W., & Associates (1957), *Behavioral goals of general education in high school*. New York: Russell Sage Foundation.

Gagné, R. M. (Ed.) (1962), *Psychological principles in system development*. New York: Holt, Rinehart and Winston.

Gagné, R. M. (1965a), Educational objectives and human performances. In J. D. Krumboltz (Ed.), *Learning and the educational process*. Chicago: Rand McNally.

Gagné, R. M. (1965b), The analysis of instructional objectives for the design of instruction. In R. Glazer (Ed.), *Teaching machines and programed learning, II*. Washington, D. C.: National Education Ass'n. of the U. S.

Gagné, R. M. (1965c), *The conditions of learning*. New York: Holt, Rinehart and Winston.

Glaser, R. (Ed.) (1962), *Training research and education*. Pittsburgh, Pa.: Univers. of Pittsburgh Press.

Glaser, R. (Ed.) (1965). *Teaching machines and programed learning, II*. Washington, D. C.: National Education Ass'n. of the U. S.

Guilford, J. P. (1967), *The nature of human intelligence*. New York: McGraw-Hill.

Horrocks, J. E. (1964), *Assessment of behavior*. Columbus, Ohio: Charles E. Merrill Books.

Kearney, N. C. (1953), *Elementary school objectives*. New York: Russell Sage Foundation.

Krathwohl, D. R., Bloom, B. S., & Masia, B. B. (1964), *Taxonomy of educational objectives – the classification of educational goals, Handbook II: affective domain.* New York: David McKay Company, Inc.

Lange, P. (Ed.) (1967), *Programed instruction.* Part II. The Sixty-sixth Yearbook of the National Society for the Study of Education. Chicago: Univers. of Chicago Press.

Lazarus, A., & Knudson, R. (1967), *Selected objectives for the english language arts: grades 7 12.* Boston: Houghton-Mifflin.

Lindvall, C. M. (Ed.) (1964), *Defining educational objectives.* Pittsburgh, Pa.: Univers. of Pittsburgh Press.

Mager, R. F. (1962), *Preparing instructional objectives.* Palo Alto, Calif.: Fearon Publishers.

Mager, R. F. (1968), *Developing attitude toward learning.* Palo Alto, Calif.: Fearon Publishers.

Mager, R. F., & Beach, K. M., Jr. (1967), *Developing vocational instruction.* Palo Alto. Calif.: Fearon Publishers.

Mager, R. F. & McCann, J. (1961), *Learner-controlled instruction.* Palo Alto, Calif.: Varian and Associates.

McCandless, B. R. (1967), *Children: behavior and development.* (2nd ed.) New York: Holt, Rinehart and Winston.

McDonald, F. J. (1965), *Educational psychology.* (2nd ed.) Belmont, Calif.: Wadsworth.

McNeil, J. D. (1966), Concomitants of using behavioral objectives in assessment of teacher effectiveness. Paper read at the American Educational Research Association Convention, Chicago.

Metfessel, N. S., Michael, W. B., & Kirsner, D. A. (1969), Instrumentation of Bloom's and Krathwohl's taxonomies for the writing of educational objectives. *Psychology in the Schools,* **6**, 227-231.

Miles, D. T., Kibler, R. J., & Pettigrew, L. E. (1967), The effects of study questions on college students' test performance. *Psychology in the Schools,* **4**, 25-26.

Miller, R. B. (1962a), Analysis and specification of behavior for training. In R. Glaser (Ed.) *Training research and education.* Pittsburgh, Pa: Univers. of Pittsburgh Press.

Miller, R. B. (1962b), Task description and analysis. In R. M. Gagné (Ed.), *Psychological principles in system development.* New York: Holt, Rinehart and Winston.

Noble, C. E. (1968), The learning of psychomotor skills, *Annual review of psychology.* **19**, 203-250.

Nunnally, J. C. (1964), *Educational measurement and evaluation.* New York: McGraw-Hill.

Payne, D. A. (1968), *The specification and measurement of learning outcomes.* Waltham, Mass.: Blaisdell.

Popham, W. J. (1965), *Systematic instructional decision making.* Los Angeles: Vimcet Associates (Audio-tape and filmstrip, 20 minutes).

Popham, W. J. (Ed.) (1969), *Instructional objectives.* Chicago: Rand McNally.

Popham, W. J., & Baker, E. (1969), *Establishing instructional goals.* Englewood Cliffs, New Jersey: Prentice-Hall.

Stolurow, L. M. (1963), *Teaching by machine.* Washington, D. C.: U. S. Government Printing Office.

Taber, J. I., Glaser, R., & Schaefer, H. H. (1965), *Learning and programmed instruction.* Reading, Mass.: Addison-Wesley.

Tyler, R. W. (1934), *Constructing achievement tests.* Columbus, Ohio: Ohio State Univers.

Tyler, R. W., Gagné, R. M. & Scriven, M. (1967), *Perspectives of curriculum evaluation.* American Educational Research Ass'n. Monograph Series on Curriculum Evaluation. Chicago: Rand McNally.

Walbesser, H. H. (1966), *Constructing behavioral objectives.* College Park, Md.: Bureau of Educational Research, Univers. of Maryland.

POSTSCRIPT

Probing the Validity of Arguments Against Behavioral Goals *

W. James Popham
University of California, Los Angeles
Southwest Regional Laboratory for Educational Research and Development

Within the last few years a rather intense debate has developed in the field of curriculum and instruction regarding the merits of stating instructional objectives in terms of measurable learner behaviors. Because I am thoroughly committed, both rationally and viscerally, to the proposition that instructional goals should be stated behaviorally, I view this debate with some ambivalence. On the one hand, it is probably desirable to have a dialogue of this sort among specialists in our field. We get to know each other better – between attacks. We test the respective worth of opposing positions. We can have hopefully stimulating symposia such as this one. Yet, as a partisan in the controversy, I would prefer unanimous support of the position to which I subscribe. You see, the other people are wrong. Adhering to a philosophic tenet that error is evil, I hate to see my friends wallowing in sin.

Moreover, their particular form of sin is more dangerous than some of the time-honored perversions of civilized societies. For example, it will probably harm more people than the most exotic forms of pornography. I believe that those who discourage educators from precisely explicating their instructional objectives are often permitting, if not promoting, the

*This paper was presented at the annual American Educational Research Association meeting, Chicago, Illinois, February 7-10, 1968. The authors are indebted to Dr. Popham and to Rand McNally and Company for granting permission to publish the paper in this volume.

same kind of unclear thinking that has led in part to the generally abysmal quality of instruction in this country.

In the remainder of this paper I shall examine eleven reasons given by my colleagues in opposition to objectives stated in terms of measurable learner behaviors. I believe each of these reasons is, for the most part, invalid. There may be minor elements of truth in some; after all, the most vile pornographer must occasionally use a few clean words. In essence, however, none of these reasons should be considered strong enough to deter educators from specifying all of their instructional goals in the precise form advocated by the "good guys" in this argument.

I shall not attempt to develop any arguments in favor of precisely stated goals, for these are treated elsewhere.[1] My only concern will be with the dubious validity of each of the following reasons.[2]

Reason one: Trivial learner behaviors are the easiest to operationalize, hence the really important outcomes of education will be underemphasized.

This particular objection to the use of precise goals is frequently voiced by educators who have recently become acquainted with the procedures for stating explicit, behavioral objectives. Since even behavioral objectives enthusiasts admit that the easiest kinds of pupil behaviors to operationalize are usually the most pedestrian, it is not surprising to find so many examples of behavioral objectives which deal with the picayune. In spite of its overall beneficial influence, the programmed booklet by Robert Mager (1962) dealing with the preparation of instructional objectives has probably suggested to many that precise objectives are usually trivial. Almost all of Mager's examples deal with cognitive behaviors which, according to Bloom's taxonomy, would be identified at the very lowest level.

Contrary to the objection raised in reason one, however, the truth is that explicit objectives make it far *easier* for educators to attend to *important* instructional outcomes. To illustrate, if you were to ask a social

[1] W. James Popham, *Educational Objectives.* Los Angeles: Vimcet Associates, 1966; W. James Popham, *Selecting Appropriate Educational Objectives.* Los Angeles: Vimcet Associates, 1967.

[2] Many of the following remarks are adapted from a symposium presentation at the 19th Annual Conference on Educational Research, California Advisory Council on Educational Research, San Diego, California, November 16, 1967.

science teacher what his objectives were for his government class and he responded as follows, "I want to make my students better citizens so that they can function effectively in our nation's dynamic democracy," you would probably find little reason to fault him. His objective sounds so profound and eminently worthwhile that few could criticize it. Yet, beneath such facades of profundity, many teachers really are aiming at extremely trivial kinds of pupil behavior changes. How often, for example, do we find "good citizenship" measured by a trifling true-false test. Now if we'd asked for the teacher's objectives in operational terms and had discovered that, indeed, all the teacher was attempting to do was promote the learner's achievement on a true-false test, we might have rejected the aim as being unimportant. But this is possible *only* with the precision of explicitly stated goals.

In other words, there is the danger that because of their ready translation to operational statements, teachers will tend to identify too many trivial behaviors as goals. But the very fact that we can make these behaviors explicit permits the teacher and his colleagues to scrutinize them carefully and thus eliminate them as unworthy of our educational efforts. Instead of encouraging unimportant outcomes in education, the use of explicit instructional objectives makes it possible to identify and reject those objectives which are unimportant.

Reason two: Prespecification of explicit goals prevents the teacher from taking advantage of instructional opportunities unexpectedly occurring in the classroom.

When one specifies explicit *ends* for an instructional program there is no necessary implication that the *means* to achieve those ends are also specified. Serendipity in the classroom is always welcome but, and here is the important point, *it should always be justified in terms of its contribution to the learner's attainment of worthwhile objectives.* Too often teachers may believe they are capitalizing on unexpected instructional opportunities in the classroom, whereas measurement of pupil growth toward any defensible criterion would demonstrate that what has happened is merely ephemeral entertainment for the pupils, temporary diversion, or some other irrelevant classroom event.

Prespecification of explicit goals does not prevent the teacher from taking advantage of unexpectedly occurring instructional opportunities in the classroom, it only tends to make the teacher justify these spontaneous learning activities in terms of worthwhile instructional ends. There are undoubtedly gifted teachers who can capitalize magnificently on the most unexpected classroom events. These teachers should not be restricted from doing so. But the teacher who prefers to probe instructional periphery, just for the sake of its spontaneity, should be deterrred by the prespecification of explicit goals.

Reason three: Besides pupil behavior changes, there are other types of educational outcomes which are important, such as changes in parental attitudes, the professional staff, community values, etc.

There are undoubtedly some fairly strong philosophic considerations associated with this particular reason. It seems reasonable that there are desirable changes to be made in our society which might be undertaken by the schools. Certainly, we would like to bring about desirable modifications in such realms as the attitudes of parents. But as a number of educational philosophers have reminded us, the schools cannot be all things to all segments of society. It seems that the primary responsibility of the schools should be to educate effectively the youth of the society. And to the extent that this is so, all modifications of parental attitudes, professional staff attitudes, etc., should be weighed in terms of a later measurable impact on the learner himself. For example, the school administrator who tells us that he wishes to bring about new kinds of attitudes on the part of his teachers should ultimately have to demonstrate that these modified attitudes result in some kind of desirable learner changes. To stop at merely modifying the behavior of teachers, without demonstrating further effects upon the learner, would be insufficient.

So while we can see that there are other types of important social outcomes to bring about, it seems that the school's primary responsibility is to its pupils. Hence, all modifications in personnel or external agencies should be justified in terms of their contribution toward the promotion of desired pupil behavior changes.

Reason four: Measurability implies behavior which can be objectively, mechanistically measured, hence there must be something dehumanizing about the approach.

This fourth reason is drawn from a long history of resistance to measurement on the grounds that it must, of necessity, reduce human learners to quantifiable bits of data. This resistance probably is most strong regarding earlier forms of measurement which were almost exclusively examination-based, and were frequently multiple-choice test measures at that. But a broadened conception of evaluation suggests that there are diverse and extremely sophisticated ways of securing qualitative as well as quantitative indices of learner performance.

One is constantly amazed to note the incredible agreement among a group of judges assigned to evaluate the complicated gyrations of skilled springboard divers in the televised reports of national aquatic championships. One of these athletes will perform an exotic, twisting dive and a few seconds after he has hit the water five or more judges raise cards reflecting their independent evaluations which can range from 0 to 10. The five ratings very frequently run as follows: 7.8, 7.6, 7.7, 7.8, and 7.5. The possibility of reliably judging something as qualitatively complicated as a springboard dive does suggest that our measurement procedures do not have to be based on a theory of reductionsim. It is currently possible to assess many complicated human behaviors in a refined fashion. Developmental work is underway in those areas where we now must rely on primitive measures.

Reason five: It is somehow undemocratic to plan in advance precisely how the learner should behave after instruction.

This particular reason was raised a few years ago in a professional journal (Arnstine, 1964) suggesting that the programmed instruction movement was basically undemocratic because it spelled out in advance how the learner was supposed to behave after instrucion. A brilliant refutation (Komisar and McClellan, 1965) appeared several months later in which the rebutting authors responded that instruction is by its very nature undemocratic and to imply that freewheeling democracy is always present in the classroom would be untruthful. Teachers generally have an idea of how they wish learners to behave, and they promote these goals with more or less efficiency. Society knows what it wants its young to become, perhaps not with the precision that we would desire, but certainly in general. And if the schools were allowing students to "democratically" deviate from societally-mandated goals, one can be sure that the institutions would cease to receive society's approbation and support.

Reason six: That isn't really the way teaching is; teachers rarely specify their goals in terms of measurable learner behaviors; so let's set realistic expectations of teachers.

Jackson (1966) recently offered this argument. He observed that teachers just don't specify their objectives in terms of measurable learner behavior and implied that, since this is the way the real world is, we ought to recognize it and live with it. Perhaps.

There is obviously a difference between identifying the status quo and applauding it. Most of us would readily concede that few teachers specify their instructional aims in terms of measurable learner behaviors, *but they ought to.* What we have to do is to mount a widespread campaign to modify this aspect of teacher behavior. Instructors must begin to identify their instructional intentions in terms of measurable learner behaviors. The way teaching really is at the moment just isn't good enough.

Reason seven: In certain subject areas, e.g., fine arts and the humanities, it is more difficult to identify measurable pupil behaviors.

Sure it's tough. Yet, because it is difficult in certain subject fields to identify measurable pupil behaviors, those subject specialists should not be allowed to escape this responsibility. Teachers in the fields of art and music often claim that it is next to impossible to identify acceptable works of art in precise terms – but they do it all the time. In instance after instance the art teacher does make a judgment regarding the acceptability of pupil-produced artwork. What the art teacher is reluctant to do is put his evaluative criteria on the line. He has such criteria. He must have to make his judgments. But he is loath to describe them in terms that anyone can see.

Any English teacher, for example, will tell you how difficult it is to make a valid judgment of a pupil's essay response. Yet criteria lurk whenever this teacher does make a judgment, and these criteria must be made explicit. No one who really understands education has ever argued that instruction is a simple task. It is even more difficult in such areas as the arts and humanities. As a noted art educator observed several years ago, art educators must quickly get to the business of specifying "tentative, but clearly defined criteria" by which they can judge their learners' artistic efforts (Munro, 1960).

Reason eight: While loose general statements of objectives may appear worthwhile to an outsider, if most educational goals were stated precisely, they would be revealed as generally innocuous.

This eighth reason contains a great deal of potential threat for school people. The unfortuante truth is that much of what is going on in the schools today is indefensible. Merely to reveal the nature of some behavior changes we are bringing about in our schools would be embarrassing. As long as general objectives are the rule, our goals may appear worthwhile to external observers. But once we start to describe precisely what kinds of changes we are bringing about in the learner, there is the danger that the public will reject our intentions as unworthy. Yet, if what we are doing is trivial, educators would know it and those who support the educational institution should also know it. To the extent that we are achieving innocuous behavior changes in learners, we are guilty. We must abandon the ploy of "obfuscation by generality" and make clear exactly what we are doing. Then we are obliged to defend our choices.

Reason nine: Measurability implies accountability; teachers might be judged on their ability to produce results in learners rather than on the many bases now used as indices of competence.

This is a particularly threatening reason and serves to produce much teacher resistence to precisely stated objectives. It doesn't take too much insight on the part of the teacher to realize that if objectives are specified in terms of measurable learner behavior, there exists the possibility that the instructor will have to become *accountable* for securing such behavior changes. Teachers might actually be judged on their ability to bring about desirable changes in learners. They should be.

But a teacher should not be judged on the particular instructional *means* he uses to bring about desirable *ends.* At present many teachers are judged adversely simply because the instructional procedures they use do not coincide with those once used by an evaluator when "he was a teacher." In other words, if I'm a supervisor who has had considerable success with open-ended discussion, I may tend to view with disfavor any teachers who cleave to more directive methods. Yet, if the teacher using the more direct methods can secure learner behavior changes which are desirable, I have no right to judge that teacher as inadequate. The possibility of assessing instructional competence in terms of the teacher's ability to bring about specified behavior changes in learners brings with it far more assets than liabilities to the teacher. He will no longer be judged on the idiosyncratic whims of a visiting supervisor. Rather, he can amass evidence that, in terms of his pupils' actual attainments, he is able to teach efficiently.

Even though this is a striking departure from the current state of affairs, and a departure that may be threatening to the less competent, the educator must promote this kind of accountability rather than the maze of folklore and mysticism which exists at the moment regarding teacher evaluation.

Reason ten: It is far more difficult to generate such precise objectives than to talk about objectives in our customarily vague terms.

Here is a very significant objection to the development of precise goals. Teachers are, for the most part, far too busy to spend the necessary hours in stating their objectives and measurement procedures with the kind of precision implied by this discussion. It is said that we are soon nearing a time when we will have more teachers than jobs. This is the time to reduce the teacher's load to the point where he can become a professional decision-maker rather than a custodian. We must reduce public school teaching loads to those of college professors. This is the time when we must give the teacher immense help in specifying his objectives. Perhaps we should *give* him objectives from which to choose, rather than force him to generate his own. Many of the federal dollars currently being used to support education would be better spent on agencies which would produce alternative behavioral objectives for all fields at all grade levels. At any rate, the difficulty of the task should not preclude its accomplishment. We can recognize how hard the job is and still allocate the necessary resources to do it.

Reason eleven: In evaluating the worth of instructional schemes it is often the unanticipated results which are really important, but prespecified goals may make the evaluator inattentive to the unforeseen.

Some fear that if we cleave to behaviorally stated objectives which must be specified prior to designing an instructional program, we will overlook certain outcomes of the program which were not anticipated yet which may be extremely important. They point out that some of the relatively recent "new curricula" in the sciences have had the unanticipated effect of sharply reducing pupil enrollments in those fields. In view of the possibility of such outcomes, both unexpectedly good and bad, it is suggested that we really ought not spell out objectives in advance, but should evaluate the adequacy of the instructional program after it has been implemented.

Such reasoning, while compelling at first glance, weakens under close scrutiny. In the first place, really dramatic unanticipated outcomes cannot be overlooked by curriculum evaluators. They certainly should not be. We should judge an instructional sequence not only by whether it attains its prespecified objectives, but also by any unforeseen consequences it produces. But what can you tell the would-be curriculum evaluator regarding this problem? "Keep your eyes open," doesn't seem to pack the desired punch. Yet, it's about all you can say. For if there is reason to believe that a particular outcome may result from an instructional sequence, it should be built into the set of objectives for the sequence. To illustrate, if the curriculum designers fear that certain negative attitudes will be acquired by the learner as he interacts with an instructional sequence, then behavioral objectives can be devised which reveal whether the instructional sequence has effectively counteracted this affective outcome. It is probably always a good idea, for example, to identify behavioral indices of the pupil's "subject-approaching tendencies." We don't want to teach youngsters how to perform mathematical exercises, for example, but to learn to hate math in the process.

Yet, it is indefensible to let an awareness of the importance of unanticipated outcomes in evaluating instructional programs lead one to the rejection of rigorous pre-planning of instructional objectives. Such objectives should be the primary, but not exclusive, focus in evaluating instruction.

While these eleven reasons are not exhaustive, they represent most of the arguments used to resist the implementation of precise instructional objectives. In spite of the very favorable overall reaction to explicit objectives during the past five to ten years, a small collection of dissident educators has arisen to oppose the quest for goal specificity. The trouble with criticisms of precise objectives isn't that they are completely without foundation. As conceded earlier, there are probably elements of truth in all of them. Yet, when we are attempting to promote the wide-scale adoption of precision in the classroom, there is the danger that many instructors will use the comments and objections of these few critics as an excuse from thinking clearly about their goals. Any risks we run by moving to behavioral goals are miniscule in contrast with our current state of confusion regarding instructional intentions. The objections against behaviorally stated goals are not strong enough. To secure a dramatic increase in instructional effectiveness we must abandon our customary practices of goal-stating and turn to a framework of precision.

References

Arnstine, D. G. (1964), The language and values of programmed instruction: part 2. *The Educational Forum, 28.*

Jackson, P. W. (1966), *The way teaching is.* Washington, D. C.: National Education Association.

Komisar, P. B., & McClellan, J. E. (1965), Professor Arnstine and programmed instruction. Reprint from *The Educational Forum.*

Mager, R. F. (1962), *Preparing instructional objectives.* San Francisco: Fearon Publishers.

Munro, T. (1960), The interrelation of the arts in secondary education. In *The creative arts in American education,* Cambridge, Mass.: Harvard University Press.

APPENDIX A

Samples of Behavioral Objectives

An efficient means of learning to write instructional objectives is to observe "models" of objectives which have been written by other teachers and curriculum planners. The purpose of this section is to provide a *variety* of such models, which encompass a wide range of subject matter, tional levels, and behavioral domains. All of the sample objectives included have been written for actual classroom use and, in most cases, have been published as part of a curriculum guide. The only exceptions are those objectives which have been written for textbooks. These also are designed indirectly for classroom use – at the discretion of the individual instructor.

The examples include a broad range of styles and formats. Some of those provided are. by no means, *behavioral* objectives. Others are very restricted behavioral objectives with little or no latitude for creativity on the part of the teacher who must execute them. The sample objectives included are not purported to be examples of "excellence" in the craft of objective formulation – they are included primarily to provide concrete examples of the types of educational objectives that are currently in use.

SCIENCE, SECONDARY SCHOOL, AFFECTIVE DOMAIN *

Awareness of Conditions

1. Relates personal requisite abilities, interest, and attitudes.
   a. Participates in extracurricular science clubs and fairs.

*National Science Supervisors Association and National Science Teachers Association, *Summary Report NSSA-NSTA Workshops on Behavioral Objectives.* Washington, D. C.: National Science Supervisors Association and National Science Teachers Association, 1967, pp. 6-15. Reprinted by permission.

b. Selects a science-related summer job.
c. Given an attitude or ability check list, can relate himself to the list as to a possible career in science.

. . .

5. Understands that science is generated by people with a compelling desire to understand the natural world.
   a. Shows interest in and respect for famous scientific biographies.
   b. Chooses a life vocation based on other than expected earning power.
   c. Selects a biography of a scientist to fulfill a book report requirement in another subject.
   d. Watches TV programs about scientists.
   e. Shows respect for the ideas of scientists.
   f. Recognizes that science is an enterprise of *human* beings.

. . .

9. Appreciates the cultural conditions under which the scientific enterprise is promoted.
   a. Accepts the concept that the social and economic climate will support or discourage the scientific enterprise.
   b. Gives logical arguments for or against national policies for the planning of research.
   c. Writes to congressmen urging support of legislation in favor of scientific research.

. . .

Acceptance of Values

10. Rejection of myths and superstitions as explanations of natural phenomena.
    a. Analyzes superstitions to see if they have scientific relevancy.
    b. Collects data to determine degree of reliability of common superstitions.

. . .

12. Has the habit of weighing evidence to formulate a considered response.
    a. Habitually consults more than one authority in searching for explanations.
    b. Identifies assumptions made as the basis of his decision-making and then questions their validity.

. . .

. . .

Preference for Values

14. Curiosity.
    a. Frequently asks questions and challenges statements of others.
    b. Asks different people the same question.
    c. Applies multi-resources to one question.
    d. Often takes a second look.
    e. Goes out of his way to find answers.
    f. Reads numerous books and magazines.
    g. Habitually examines the working parts of equipment being used.
    h. Visits museums and industrial or food-processing plants.
    i. Initiates questions voluntarily.
    j. Exhibits awareness of discrepancies in his environment.
    k. Collects and orders the collection in some way.
    l. Includes reading about science and watching science-based programs in leisure time activities.
    m. Uses all senses in making observations.

. . .

16. Persistence.
    a. Is willing to repeat an effort voluntarily.
    b. Redesigns experimental systems in an attempt to improve results.
17. Open-mindedness.
    a. Listens carefully when others are talking.
    b. Insists on hearing more than one opinion on one piece of evidence.
    c. Is willing to change ideas when new or additional evidence is available.
    d. Will give consideration to ideas which differ from his own.

. . .

20. Confidence in the scientific method.
    a. Follows instructions of doctor.
    b. Cleans out medicine closet periodically.
    c. Attempts to use scientific methods when making decisions.
    d. Looks for data or evidence before acting.
    e. Consults and considers consumer reports.
    f. Votes for elected officials on the basis of available evidence.

. . .

27. The desire to be creative.

a. Participates in research on his own initiative.
b. Offers realistic alternatives to a presented method for doing something.
c. Gets involved in independent study.
d. Displays a variety of reactions or insights.

. . .

SCIENCE, JR. HIGH SCHOOL, COGNITIVE AND AFFECTIVE DOMAINS*

. . .

To Develop Rational Thinking Powers Which Underlie Scientific Modes of Inquiry.

. . .

3. Generate data to support or refine theories.

   When provided with a microscope and yeast culture and asked to provide data that supports their theory that yeast is alive because it is made up of cells that grow and reproduce, the students observe growth and splitting off of buds, record observations in a series of drawings, or describe the sequence of events in writing.

. . .

6. Generalize the usefulness of theories which they have derived into a broader concept.

   Given a thermostat (or diagram of a thermostat) containing a compound metal bar, the students explain how it works in terms of their previously verified theory used to explain the bending of a bimetallic strip when heated.

. . .

To Develop Those Scientific Values, Appreciations, and Attitudes Which Underlie the Personal Involvement of an Individual as He Investigates the Environment and Mankind.

1. Are intrigued by phenomena in the environment.

   When seeking explanations for objects and events, the students: examine objects carefully, ask relevant questions, use a combination of senses to collect data, volunteer to change the conditions in which the event took place, look for problems and note discrepancies, persist

*A. N. Gentry, Ed., *Planning a Continuous Science Program for All Junior High School Youth.* Riverside, California: Office of the Superintendent of Schools, pp. 60-64. Reprinted by permission.

in seeking causes for events which are not immediately apparent, see and point out discrepancies which others do not see, tolerate periods of time when there is conflicting and incomplete data.

2. Exhibit enjoyment in processing data, building theories, and seeking concepts.

   When approaching new ideas, the students: exhibit an interest in unfamiliar phenomena, formulate opinions only after seeking a variety of data and ideas, show that they are willing to change their theories in the light of new evidence, suggest original explanations for a puzzling event, seek and consider explanatory ideas of others, test theories of others which disagree with their own, show evidence of exhilaration when finding agreement between theory and data, seek opportunities to share their ideas about the mysteries of the universe with others, express feelings of satisfaction and pleasure in seeing complexity expressed in a simple form.

3. Show appreciation for the rational nature of science.

   During post-lab evaluations, the students: suggest logical explanations for events, point out contradictions between data and theory, criticize explanations which cannot be tested in a rational way.

   The students seek and read books which describe the creative genius of scholarly scientific works of the past and present.

4. Interact with others in building theories and seeking data during laboratory investigations and reporting and discussion periods.

   During group and class discussions the students: volunteer their data and ideas, listen critically to explanations of others, read what others have reported, show willingness to expose their tentative ideas and explanations to others and seek their criticism, refrain from anger or defensiveness when criticized, introduce controversial issues into the discussion when appropriate.

   The students: offer to collaborate with others on ideas, projects, and activities of common interest; volunteer to make oral and written reports.

5. Demonstrate personal integrity when reporting their work.

   When presenting oral and written reports and writing laboratory and field data logs, the students: report data which conflict with their own theories, give credit to others whenever due, admit their mistakes, point out the limitations of their data, log only those data which they actually gathered.

6. Respond to beauty in the environment.

   When asked to express their own way, their feelings about what they have observed in nature, the students: express their consciousness and/or pleasure in color, form, texture, arrangement, or design of objects in the environment by means of oral or written descriptions, poems, drawings, paintings, sculpture, and the like.

   When observing and investigating the environment, the students: search and report evidences of order, symmetry, and precision.

. . .

To Develop Fundamental Skills Involved in Procuring, Recording, Organizing, Interpreting, and Reporting Scientific Information and the Linguistic Skills That Enhance the Communication of Ideas.

. . .

3. Precisely and accurately record observations and ideas for use in theory building and concept formation.

   When recording data obtained from observations and investigations, the students: make simple diagrams which illustrate objects, events, or concepts; keep written logs of observations; record quantitative data in tabular or other suitable form; represent ideas graphically; use precise and unambiguous language to describe observations; organize recorded data in a manner that enhances their subsequent interpretation.

. . .

5. Use recognized library research skills to extend their knowledge of the accomplishments and the unsolved problems of science.

   When obtaining information and ideas from the library, the students: use card catalogue and other standard references sources; use other resources when information is not available in school or community library; document statements and opinions; consider recency of publications and competency of author; use original sources, when available.

6. Use appropriate mathematical tools, symbols, and operations to describe, interpret, and organize data to communicate ideas in a precise manner.

   When conducting and reporting laboratory investigations and observations, the students: use quantitative terms to describe observations; use metric measurements; use scientific notation in recording and reporting very large and very small numbers; use pictures and diagrams to indicate actual size of objects when the scale is given; graph ordered pairs of data; predict from graphs by extrapolation; infer the equation for a straight line graph; represent ideas in the form of mathematical models; apply operations of arithmetic and simple algebra to science problems and data processing.

. . .

To Develop Basic Understandings of Terminology, Concepts, and Procedures Which Further the Processes of Interpreting Phenomena, Predicting and Controlling Events, and Generating More Powerful Theories.

. . .

1. Demonstrate knowledge and comprehension of scientific terminology and specific facts which have been emphasized in the junior high school curriculum.

   When shown a familiar diagram of a plant cell, the students identify correctly at least seven of the following parts: chloroplast, cell wall, plasma membrane, cytoplasm, Golgi apparatus, mitochondria, nucleolus, chromatin, plastid, nuclear membrane.

   When asked to define a list of key terms (*i.e.*, atom, biosphere, catalyst, diffusion, energy, substance, solution) the students state acceptable operational definitions for at least 70 percent of the terms.

2. Demonstrate knowledge of ways and means of dealing with specifics (knowledge of the ways of organizing, studying, judging, and criticizing).

When given the names of ten previously encountered organisms, the students classify at least seven of them under the proper kingdom, phylum, and class.

When given previously unencountered hypotheses about environmental phenomena, the students describe one or more appropriate methods for testing each hypothesis.

. . .

4. Describe major theories and structures of science.

When asked to describe how classification of living things provides evidence to support the theory of evolution, the students state that intergrading forms of plants and animals differing from earlier species indicate that evolutionary change is probably taking place today in living things.

. . .

5. Demonstrate knowledge of relationships between science and society.

In a social studies class the students give examples of new technologies and/or science breakthroughs which resulted in changes in the way we live.

. . . .

SECONDARY TEACHER EDUCATION, COLLEGE, COGNITIVE AND AFFECTIVE DOMAINS*

Preassessment.

. . .

Given or having written behavioral objectives and conceptual or skill statements, the pre-service teacher will write appropriate preassessment procedures which:

a. Determine that the learner can or cannot perform the behavior of the objectives, or;
b. That he has a working knowledge of the concepts or skills requisite to performance of the behavior of the objectives.

. . .

*Vere A. McHenry, Ed., "The Individualized Secondary Teacher Education Program at Brigham Young University," *M-STEP Monograph,* No. 2, Salt Lake City: Utah State Board of Education, pp. 7, 8, 10, 11, 13, 14, 16, 21-23, 28 and 29. Reprinted by permission.

Teaching Methods.

. . .

The pre-service teacher will demonstrate the instructional use of role playing, dramatization and pantomine, buzz and discussion groups, panels and committees. Demonstrations will be done by team presentations and must include the following:

a. Use of assigned equipment.
b. Instruction in how to prepare pupils to use and benefit from the method.
c. Relevant cautions regarding use of the method.
d. Learning activities which will help members of the college class apply the method to their respective subject area.

Creativity, imagination, and a fresh kind of presentation will not be penalized.

. . .

Human Development.

. . .

The pre-service teacher will, upon being presented with descriptions of a variety of human behaviors often exhibited by particular age groups in a closed book essay examination:

a. Analyze the situation and state the factors according to human development principles, which appear to be causing or contributing to the problem.
b. From the descriptions of predominant developmental characteristics (emotional, social, intellectual, and physical), hypothesize the major problem(s) for which there should be concern.
c. Propose in writing various alternatives based upon his knowledge of human development principles that a teacher and/or parent might utilize to lessen the concern of those acting to solve the problem(s).

. . .

16 MM Projector.

. . .

The pre-service teacher will operate an autoload and two other types of 16 mm projectors. Operate includes assembling the equipment, threading the film, adjusting the sound and visual image, rewinding the film, storing the equipment, and preparing the room.

Preparing the equipment and the room should take no more than five minutes.

. . .

Behavioral Objectives.

. . .

The pre-service teacher will write at least nine educational objectives which are behavioral according to Mager's (1962) criteria, at least three of which would be classified in each of the following categories: affective, higher than lowest cognitive, and psychomotor.

a. Objectives for at least two of these categories in your major or minor fields.
b. The three objectives in the higher than lowest cognitive category in a sequence in order that one behavior leads to the next.
c. Label the parts of at least three of the nine objectives according to the criteria identified by Mager.

. . .

Micro-Teaching: Teach a Concept.

. . .

The pre-service teacher will teach a single concept and evaluate whether or not it has been learned within a period of seven minutes. A critique of the presentation will be made by the class members in terms of the learning activities selected to bring the referent to the students, amount of student involvement, whether or not the concept was learned, and the voice, poise, and mannerisms of the teacher. He will summarize the suggestions made for improvement and state those he would select for implementation and the steps he would take to implement them.

. . .

Micro-Teaching: Reinforcing Student Behavior.

. . .

While teaching a seven-minute concept lesson, the pre-service teacher will demonstrate positive ways to reinforce desirable student behavior. The demonstration will include at least four different appropriate ways of providing positive reinforcement and must involve directly a majority of the members of the micro-class.

. . .

Cognitive Learning Sequence.

. . .

For all assigned lesson plans and curriculum units, the pre-service teacher will prepare learning activities to do the following:

a. Focus the attention of the learners on the referent for each major concept.
b. Provide for conceptualization of each major concept at *and* above the lowest cognitive level.
c. Make provisions for application of each major concept by the learners.

Upon being given a specific teaching-learning situation, the pre-service teacher will be able to differentiate between appropriate sequential teaching procedures for cognitive learning by specifically outlining during a timed, open book test, those appropriate teaching procedures to achieve the intended objective.

To be acceptable, the three steps in the learning sequence must occur in the order listed above.

. . .

Test Construction and Analysis.

. . .

The pre-service teacher will construct a test instrument which contains at least three examples of each type of test question and which specifically measures achievement of terminal behavior specified in a unit for which he has major responsibility, such that at least 10% of the items call for student response above the lowest cognitive level.

. . .

Discipline Interaction.

. . .

The pre-service teacher will listen to a taped classroom situation involving a discipline problem and after analysis write a dialogue demonstrating alternative teacher behavior which is less of a personal affront and thus more behavior oriented, "supportive rather than rejectory," and "non-threatening" as identified by Amidon and Hunter.

Student Teaching: Class Orientation.

. . .

The pre-service teacher will prepare and present an orientation to his student which will communicate his intent regarding each of the following:

a. Format and materials for recording written assignments.
b. Course, content, and behavioral objectives.
c. Types of learning activities to be used for student involvement.
d. Types of materials and resources to be drawn upon the learning activities.
e. Evaluative procedures to be used.
f. The grading system to be followed.

Effectiveness of presentation is to be judged by team members and also by students during pupil evaluation sessions.

. . .

Affective Behaviors: Teacher Role Perception.

. . .

Upon completion of the program a majority of the students will have changed their perception of the role of the secondary teacher. End-of-course perception will have moved toward the right, assuming a continuum of role perception moving from the left end where the teacher is seen as an "authoritarian teller" to the right end where the teacher is seen as a non-directive resource person.

Role perception will be measured with pre- and post-instruments and observations.

. . .

Affective Behaviors: Individualized Instruction and Evaluative Criteria.

. . .

Upon completion of the Secondary Experimental Program, the pre-service teacher will demonstrate his preference for individualized instruction by doing at least one of the following in his first year of teaching:

a. Use at least ten techniques to provide for individual differences.
b. Design at least three units to allow students to proceed at their best pace.
c. Allow students in at least one class to pursue areas of their own interest for one-fourth of the year's work.

Upon completion of the Secondary Experimental Program, the pre-service teacher will demonstrate his preference for criterion-referenced evaluation by basing the evaluation of student achievement on these procedures at least 75% of the time during his first year of teaching.

. . .

ECONOMICS, COLLEGE, COGNITIVE DOMAIN*

Understand the changing relationships between money income and real income as prices change:

1. Recognize that when income is expressed in terms of "constant dollars" the influence of changes in prices has been eliminated from the income figures.
2. Recognize that an increase in the price level tends to redistribute purchasing power, *e.g.*, diminishes the real income of those on fixed incomes and influences other people variously.
3. Recognize that a decrease in the price level tends to redistribute purchasing power, *e.g.*, increases the real income of individuals with fixed income, etc.

Distinguish between an inflationary and a deflationary gap:

1. Recognize that a deflationary gap exists when aggregate demand is not sufficient to sustain full employment in the economy.
2. Recognize that an inflationary gap exists when aggregate demand exceeds the value of the output possible with full employment (in terms of current prices).

Understand the processes by which an inflationary or deflationary gap is eliminated:

1. Identify an increase in aggregate demand as a means of closing or eliminating a deflationary gap.

*P. W. Tiemann, "Outcomes in a Televised College Economics Course with Variable Student Knowledge of Objectives," Doctoral dissertation, University of Illinois, 1967, pp. 152-154. (Course Director: D. W. Paden, Professor of Economics, University of Illinois). Reprinted by permission.

2. Identify a decrease in aggregate demand as a means of closing or eliminating an inflationary gap.

Understand what happens in the event an inflationary or deflationary gap (caused by investment expenditures) is not eliminated:

1. Recall that an increase in the level of prices resulting from an inflationary gap brings about a redistribution of income [see objective 2 of "Understand the changing relationship..."].
2. Given an inflationary gap, recognize that a new equilibrium level of income may be possible (as prices rise) only if sufficient saving is generated through the resulting redistribution of income to match the higher level of investment.
3. Recall that a decrease in the level of prices resulting from a deflationary gap brings about a redistribution of income [see objective 3 of "Understanding the changing relationship..."].
4. Recognize that as output decreases and unemployment increases, savings decline.
5. Given a deflationary gap recognize that a new equilibrium level of income will be reached only when saving decreases sufficiently to be equal to the lower level of investment.

Understand what happens in the event an inflationary gap (caused by government expenditures) is *not* eliminated:

1. Recognize that an increase in government expenditure may be responsible for an inflationary gap.
2. Recognize that a new equilibrium level of income may be possible only if sufficient tax receipts and/or saving is generated as a result of income and price changes to match the high level of government expenditure.

Understand the relationship between increasing expenditures and full employment:

1. Indicate that *output* will tend to rise as a result of an increase in total expenditures (C+I+G) when the economy is initially operating at *less than* full employment.

2. Indicate that *prices* will tend to rise as a result of an increase in total expenditures when the economy is initially operating *at* full employment (given a situation of full employment, output is not able to rise much beyond full employment capacity).

Know what is meant by the consumer price index and how to interpret the index:

1. For the period 1929-1933, identify a rapid decline in the consumer price index with a rapid increase in unemployment and a substantial decline in output.
2. For the period 1934-1941, identify a gradual increase in the consumer price index with a gradual decrease in unemployment and a substantial increase in output – remembering that the economy was operating at less than full employment.
3. For the period 1946-1948, identify a rapid increase in the consumer price index with an almost constant output – remembering that the economy was operating near full employment.

Know how an inflationary or deflationary gap is represented on an income and expenditure chart:

1. Given an income and expenditure chart showing (1) actual aggregate demand and (2) the threatened level of aggregate demand, indicate the value of the inflationary (or deflationary) gap.
2. Given the same situation, identify the amount by which aggregate demand must be decreased (or increased) in order to eliminate the gap.
3. Compute the inflationary or deflationary gap given the (1) actual or anticipated equilibrium level of income, (2) the full employment level of income, and (3) a relevant marginal propensity to consume.

Understand what is meant by cost-push inflation:

1. Recognize that cost-push inflation may occur in spite of a deficiency in aggregate demand.
2. Identify cost-push inflation with the presence of monopoly power which tends to push the costs of goods and services upward without parallel increases in productivity.

EDUCATIONAL PSYCHOLOGY, COLLEGE, COGNITIVE DOMAIN*

Upon reading the first section of this chapter (on a theory of teaching), you should be able to meet these objectives:

1. Indicate the three questions about teaching behavior which a theory of teaching answers and provide an illustration of a theory of teaching which raises and answers these questions.
2. Point out characteristics (in terms of questions raised and answered) which distinguish a theory of teaching from a theory of learning; describe the relationship between a theory of teaching and a theory of learning; and provide illustrations of a theory of teaching and of a theory of learning which indicate these distinctions and relationships.
3. Point out characteristics (in terms of questions raised and answered) which distinguish a theory of teaching from a philosophy of education; illustrate these distinctions by comparing a teaching theory and a philosophy of education.

Upon reading the second and third sections of this chapter (on models of teaching), you should be able to meet these objectives:

4. List the four components of the basic teaching model and illustrate how a feedback loop from performance assessment (the fourth component) results in adjustments in the three remaining components.
5. Describe the psychological teaching models of (a) Stolurow, (b) Carroll, and (c) Flanders in terms of the components of the basic teaching model.
6. Describe the historical teaching models of (a) Socrates, (b) the Jesuits, and (c) Combs and Snygg in terms of the components of the basic teaching model.

. . .

Upon reading the first section of this chapter (on the definition of entering behavior), you should be able to meet these objectives:

*John P. DeCecco, *The Psychology of Learning and Instruction: Educational Psychology*.© 1968. Reprinted by permission of Prentice-Hall, Inc., Englewood Cliffs, New Jersey, pp. 5 and 6, 57 and 58, 85, 128 and 129, 242, 430, 485 and 486, and 701 and 702.

1. List the major characteristics of entering behavior.
2. Distinguish entering behavior from and relate it to terminal performance by pointing out similar and dissimilar characteristics.
3. Distinguish entering behavior from and relate it to readiness, maturation, individual differences, and personality by pointing out similar and dissimilar characteristics.
4. Illustrate relevant entering behavior for an instructional objective of your own choice.

. . .

Upon reading the second section of this chapter (on the measurement of intelligence), you should be able to meet these objectives:

. . .

13. Distinguish among the three types of intelligence tests: individual tests, group tests, and test batteries; point out the assets and limitations of each type; illustrate appropriate uses of each type.

. . .

19. List the practical limitations of IQ tests and show how these could be reduced by the appropriate anlysis of intellectual processes; indicate how IQ becomes a better predictor of school achievement as we increase our precision in describing entering behavior and as we improve the quality of instruction.

. . .

Upon reading the first section of this chapter (on the definition of motivation), you should be able to meet these objectives:

1. List the characteristics of the concept of motivation and distinguish between behavior which is best explained in terms of motivation and behavior which is best explained in terms of habits, abilities, external stimuli, and so on.

. . .

9. Define incentives and explain and illustrate how they increase response vigor; distinguish between positive and negative reinforcers and aversive stimuli and describe their influence in imitative learning.

10. Distinguish between escape and avoidance training and a punishment procedure; explain how punishment is related to intensity of shock, to

a rewarded alternative, and to consumatory responses; describe and illustrate two psychological myths about the effects of punishment.

11. Distinguish between the model of motivation offered in this chapter and those of drive-reduction theory, of Freudian theory, and of self-actualizing tendencies.

. . .

Upon reading the first section of this chapter (on a definition of learning), you should be able to meet these objectives:

1. Define learning in terms of change, reinforcement, and practice.
2. Distinguish learning from performance, native response tendencies, maturation, and temporary states of the organism.
3. Define the learning event in terms of stimulus, response, and learner, and provide illustrations of learning events.

. . .

Upon reading the third section of this chapter (on instruction for creativity), you should be able to meet these objectives:

14. Define and illustrate creative abilities in terms of flexibility, originality, and fluency.

. . .

21. Describe and illustrate the use of research skills and creative reading in creative problem solving.
22. Describe and illustrate the ways in which the teacher can reward creative achievement.

. . .

Upon reading the first section of this chapter (on programed instruction), you should be able to meet these objectives:

3. Describe and illustrate each of the following steps in the preparation of a program: (a) select a unit or topic; (b) prepare a content outline: (c) define your objectives in behavioral terms; (d) construct a test of entering behavior; and (e) construct a test of terminal behavior.

. . .

15. Point out and diagrammatically illustrate the similarities and differences in these three types of programs: (a) linear, (b) branching, and (c) adjunct autoinstructional.
16. Describe how you would obtain information to answer each of the following questions in the selection of a program: (a) Is it really programed material? (b) How does the program fit into the curriculum? (c) How well will the program teach in your situation? (d) Can you afford it?

. . .

Upon reading the third section of this chapter (on the analysis of data), you should be able to meet these objectives:

16. Define and illustrate the null hypothesis and distinguish it from the research hypothesis.
17. Define statistical significance and explain $p = 0.01$, $p = 0.05$, and $p = 0.001$.

. . .

19. Define and illustrate the appropriate use of the F ratio and compute the F ratio when given the mean square between groups and the mean square within groups.

. . .

21. Distinguish and illustrate the differences between parametric and non-parametric tests.
22. Define and illustrate the use of factor analysis as a means of finding common variables.

ELEMENTARY STATISTICS, COLLEGE, COGNITIVE DOMAIN*

Objectives for the study of constants and variables:

1. Recognize and recall (R & R) that a constant is a quantity that has a fixed value – a single numerical value. This value may sometimes be unknown, but if known, it can be represented by a single number.

*Paul A. Games and George R. Klare, *Elementary Statistics: Data Analysis for the Behavioral Sciences.* New York: McGraw-Hill Book Company, 1967, pp. 8, 12, 14 and 20-21. Reprinted by permission.

2. R & R that constants are symbolized by one of the first three letters of the alphabet, plus *K* (for "konstant"), in lower-case-letter format: a, b, c, or k.
3. R & R that a variable is a quantity that may take any of a set of values – that is, it can have many numerical values.
4. R & R that in general, variables are symbolized by one of the last six letters of the alphabet in either capital-letter format (U, V, W, X, Y, or Z) or lower-case-letter format (u, v, w, x, y, or z). Symbols for special statistical indices that are variables will be separately defined where needed.
5. R & R that a set of numerical data can be represented as X:1, 3, 3, 4, 6, 8, etc. This means (and is read as) X takes the values 1, 3, 3, etc.

. . .

Objectives for the study of populations and samples:

1. R & R (recognize and recall) that a population is defined as a complete set of objects or observations, and that N refers to the number in the set.
2. R & R that a sample is defined as a subset of population, or as an incomplete set of objects or observations, and that *n* refers to the number of cases in the subset.
3. Recognize there are two situations, with the latter (observations) more common:
   (a) populations or samples of objects (persons, animals, plants, etc.);
   (b) populations or samples of observations.
4. Recognize the populations involved in some well-specified scientific questions.
5. Distinguish whether a set of data is a sample or a population from the verbal description of the question and the data.
6. Recognize that a set of data may be considered either population or sample, depending upon the question asked by the experimenter.
7. R & R that one population may contain many samples. Population data are stable, fixed, and unvarying, since all measures are included; sample data vary (fluctuate) from one sample to another, and are therefore somewhat unstable.

8. R & R that the larger the sample size, the smaller the variation from one sample to another; chance differences between sample characteristics and population characteristics are smaller with a larger n.

. . .

Objectives for the study of parameters and statistics:

1. R & R the definition of parameters and statistics:
   (a) A parameter is a descriptive index of a population;
   (b) A statistic is a descriptive index of a sample.
2. R & R that:
   (a) parameters have the characteristics of a population – they are stable, fixed, unvarying;
   (b) statistics have the characteristics of a sample – they fluctuate from one sample to another.
3. R & R that the larger the sampling size n, the smaller the sampling fluctuation of the statistic.
4. Recognize that most scientific questions are about parameters; therefore, the goal of scientific investigation is to obtain information about parameters.
5. R & R that if population data are *not* available, a sample must be drawn, a *statistic* computed to provide a *descriptive* value, and *inference* used to reach conclusions about the parameter.
6. R & R that if population data are available, the *parameter* may be computed directly, and the *descriptive* value is thus obtained.
7. R & R that:
   (a) parameters are symbolized by capital or Greek letters – P, (sigma), (mu), etc.;
   (b) statistics are symbolized by lower-case letters – p, s, etc.
8. R & R the interpretation of subscripts; read x as "mu sub X" and interpret it as the population mean of the variable X.

. . .

Objectives for the study of types of data:

1. Distinguish between categorical, ranked, and metric measures.
   (a) Observations that may only be placed in different classes or categories are referred to as categorical data.

(b) Observations that only express relative position in a group (first, second, etc.) are referred to as ranked data.

(c) Observations secured by a process that assigns a given number to a response regardless of what other responses may have been made are referred to as metric data.

2. Recognize that the authors of this text do not believe that the distinction between nominal, ordinal, interval, and ratio scales is very helpful in deciding upon the proper statistical techniques to use in the behavioral sciences (note that definition of these scales is *not* an Objective).
3. Distinguish between continuous and discrete metric measures.
   (a) Discrete measures can only fall at certain separated points on a scale.
   (b) Continuous measures are not limited to specified points, but may have any possible value.
4. R & R that in this course all metric data will be considered to be a discrete approximation to a continuous measure; a given numerical value will be thought of as the midpoint of an interval on a continuous measure.
5. R & R that all numerical metric data will be referred to as "scores" regardless of the scale on which they are obtained (*e.g.*, pounds, inches, IQs, etc.).
6. Recognize that the uses of statistics and parameters are not specific to a particular type of metric data, nor is the derivation of the metric data a matter of *statistical* concern. The derivation of the data is of great *scientific* concern, since it determines what interpretations are justified. It is simply that the theory of statistics works impartially well on any set of metric data.

COMMUNICATION OBJECTIVES FOR COLLEGE, COGNITIVE AND PSYCHOMOTOR DOMAINS*

OBJECTIVES FOR NONVERBAL COMMUNICATION

After studying this chapter, you should be better able to do these things:

*From *Interpersonal Speech Communication* by John Keltner, a forthcoming publication by Wadsworth Publishing Company, Inc., Belmont, California. All rights reserved. By permission.

1. Recognize nonverbal messages that are sent during a speech-communication event.
2. Identify many of the nonverbal messages that are parts of a culture.
3. Realize that it is almost impossible to avoid communicating.
4. Identify sign, action, and object languages.
5. Recognize the metacommunication systems in speech-communication.
6. Perceive mixed messages and their effect on communication efforts.
7. Focus on nonverbal messages that are often concealed by verbal messages.
8. Develop an awareness of the effect of pitch, quality, volume, and rate on the tonal code in communication.
9. Identify bodily movements that convey meanings consistent with and contradictory to verbal messages.
10. Use bodily activity to send messages without verbal reinforcement.
11. Realize the importance of freeing the body of tensions and restraints so that it may become an effective tool in nonverbal communication and in the reinforcement of verbal communication.
12. Recognize that bodily movement and action comes from internal feelings that are associated with the basic message involved in the communication event.
13. Perceive the effect of distance or space as a cue in communicating messages.
14. Recognize that timing and rhythm are also cues that may tell much as part of a total communication effort.
15. Become sensitive to the many nonverbal systems that make up the supporting behavior to speech-communication.

. . .

OBJECTIVES FOR DECISION-MAKING, COMMITMENT, AND PROBLEM-SOLVING

After studying this chapter, you should be better able to do these things:

1. Distinguish between decision-making and problem-solving.
2. Recognize decisions as commitments.
3. Realize that everyone is constantly making decisions.
4. Perceive attitudes as arrangements of decisions relating to some reference point.

5. Understand how personal decisions and *agreements* between people are related.
6. Distinguish between valid and phony agreements.
7. Realize that your decisions are determined by your goals, needs, group pressures, rationalizations, and authority.
8. Resist group pressures to agree when agreement is contrary to your own personal decisions.
9. Test the credibility of "authorities" who seek to persuade you to accept their decisions as your own.
10. Realize the difficulties involved as two or more people reach a joint decision.
11. Identify problems more effectively.
12. Understand that problem-solving involves a series of decisions.
13. Separate the elements of a problem in order to deal with it more effectively.
14. Seek to recognize and identify your goals and the obstacles you face in achieving them.
15. Realize the difference between general and specific goals.
16. Define the point at which goals and obstacles meet (point of encounter).
17. Solve problems more efficiently both alone and as a member of a group.
18. Distinguish between a problem and its solution.
19. Set up clear criteria for the solution to a problem.
20. Establish several alternative solutions for consideration when trying to solve a problem.
21. Work more effectively in a problem-solving group.

ENGLISH LANGUAGE ARTS, HIGH SCHOOL, AFFECTIVE DOMAIN*

Objectives related to attitudes about readings:

1. to enjoy reading.
2. to believe that everone's reading can be improved.

*Arnold Lazarus and Rozanne Knudson, *Selected Objectives for the English Language Arts Grades 7-12.* Boston: Houghton Mifflin Company, 1967, pp. 17, 18, 36, 45, 71 and 79-80. Reprinted by permission.

3. to be committed to reading as a lifetime experience and to Francis Bacon's observation that "Reading maketh a full man."
4. to enjoy library visits; to cherish the library as a civilizing institution.
5. to desire the knowledge, insight, and aesthetic appreciation that one can get from reading many different kinds of books and periodicals.
6. to appreciate the talent and skill of professional writers; to savor, in one's reading, the surprisingly apt expression.
7. to prefer, more often than not, serious reading to "entertainment"; yet to accept one's need for an occasional change of pace (to be willing to read detective stories, for example, or "light" novels or verse).
8. to recognize the importance of reading in democratic living; to value reading as a way of becoming better informed and thus better able to participate more intelligently in democratic institutions.

. . .

Objectives related to attitudes about poetry:

1. to respect poetry as a priceless art form, as something that may heighten one's sensitivity to living.
2. to accept the fact that poetry is essentially secular and hedonistic – that it celebrates things of this world, as John Crow Ransom and others have observed.
3. to regard as possible treasures the poems one likes now, but to be willing to reasses this treasury, from time to time, subjecting it to one's changing tastes.
4. to appreciate the beauty of sound in poetry, and the relationship between sound and sense.
5. to enjoy discovering the paradoxes and planned ambiguities of poems.

. . .

Objectives related to attitudes about drama:

1. to respect drama as an art form to be seen and heard rather than just read.
2. to desire to grow in one's understanding and appreciation of drama.
3. to accept the continuum of quality in drama; to be aware of the fact that there are many plays that may be watched, heard, and read to develop taste as well as for enjoyment.

4. to relish complications of situation and character; to enjoy the rising suspensive action of dramas and their denouements.

. . .

Objectives related to attitudes about spelling:

1. to become sensitive (preferably before Grade 7) to the fact that communications containing misspellings *look* illiterate.
2. to value correct spelling; to desire to become an efficient speller; to deplore poor spelling as a demonstration of laziness.
3. to believe that almost anyone can learn to spell; that facility in spelling is not something one is born with; that it is achieved only through patient study and practice.
4. to be willing to consult a dictionary when in doubt about a word.

. . .

Objectives related to attitudes about writing:

1. to respect utilitarian writing tasks; to realize that some of the world's work, as specified below under "understandings" and "skills," often depends on one's careful treatment of even the most unglamourous kind of writing assignment (*e.g.*, notes itemizing goods received).
2. to take satisfaction in the sense of orderliness that is part of efficiently carrying out utilitarian writing tasks.
3. to want to be articulate, accurate, and truthful in even the most common everyday writing task.
4. to be willing to teach oneself on one's own time most of the conventions of utilitarian writing (notes, business letters, classified advertisements); to respect the preference of most English-teachers to spend the majority of class time on more important matters such as expository writing and the study of literature.

ESTHETIC DEVELOPMENT, ELEMENTARY, PSYCHOMOTOR DOMAIN*

Skill and Competence in Esthetic Development

Primary Period. He knows how to use simple rhythm instruments. He can skip to music in unison with others, clap hands to the rhythmic patterns of a new song, keep step to music, interpret rhythm through bodily movements, quickly grasp the melody of a song, sing in tune without the piano, discover new tunes and patterns in music, and sing a few songs if provided with the words.

He is able to draw and paint, with some realism and detail, but – more important – with satisfaction to himself, the simple things that strike his fancy, such as trees, animals, and human figures. He uses pencils, crayons, paints, finger paints. He can create simple designs or reproduce them from memory. He can use margins in mountings, in written papers, and so on. He can use clay in simple pottery forms. He can weave simple mats and make simple constructions with paper, cardboard, metal.

He can listen to and observe, or plan to take part in, a dramatization. He can detect rhythms in poetry. He can derive meaning from poems concerning child life. He is developing skill in using his small muscles in the arts and crafts.

. . .

Intermediate Period. He has some of the skills necessary for art work in connection with study themes; for example, making pottery, pictorial maps, murals, decorative fabrics, stage settings, puppets, dioramas. He can select appropriate music for programs. He has skill in such crafts as ceramics, metalwork, leatherwork, wood- or soap-carving. He can reproduce in imagination the sights, sounds, smells, feelings, and tastes suggested in stories and programs. He can folk dance in figures and sets – combining rhythm and muscle control.

He is able to read a simple melody, reproduce with voice or instrument the music he can read, blend his voice in part or unison singing, and play

*Nolan C. Kearney, *Elementary School Objectives.* New York: Russell Sage Foundation, 1953, pp. 97-99. Reprinted by permission.

some simple musical instrument. He can operate recorders, wire or tape machines, and the like that are available in his school. He knows how to make musical instruments from simple materials.

He can follow the story in simple narrative poems and recognize allegory with little or no interpretation. His skill in expressing dramatic experiences is increasing.

He has some skill in many of the graphic arts. He tries to be accurate in drawing and uses shading to show depth. He knows how to select clothing, and chooses colors for a room or for a painting with some skill in use of hues, value, intensity, harmony. He applies esthetic principles in making airplane and boat models. He evaluates radio and television shows critically.

. . .

Upper-Grade Period. He is able to apply the principles of design and color combination in such situations as buying and wearing clothing, planning a home, interior decorating, redecorating, drawing a plan in perspective, drawing a room's interior, and arranging furniture.

He is able to suggest appropriate music for various occasions. He exercises creativity in suggesting (and sometimes helping to compose) music for songs, dances, and instruments. He is able to read music for singing, sings well enough to gain satisfaction from it, and otherwise participates with enjoyment in musical experiences. He is able to play an instrument, whirl a baton, or perform some skill of a like nature. He is able to respond to changes of rhythm in music and dancing.

He has skill in woodcarving, needlework, beadwork, leatherwork, and other crafts. He uses discrimination in his "consumption" of motion pictures, radio, television, comics. He can apply standards of beauty and design in writing, drawing, and so on.

GENERAL EDUCATION-SOCIAL STUDIES, HIGH SCHOOL, AFFECTIVE DOMAIN*

Appreciates Opportunities for Cultural and Intellectual Activities within the Family:

1. Has the ability to entertain other members of his family and friends in

*Will French and Associates, *Behavioral Goals of General Education in High School.* New York: Russell Sage Foundation, 1957, p. 147. Reprinted by permission.

ways consistent with the resources available and his family situation.
2. Cooperates in the gradual building of a well-chosen home library.
3. Discovers books and magazine articles on subjects of interest to members of the family and calls them to their attention.
4. Takes pride in the good appearance of his home, neighborhood, and community.
5. Is interested in taking part in discussions of, and helps in work concerned with, beautifying the home.
6. Understands the purpose of zoning laws and supports them.
7. Seeks increasing opportunity for expanding his creative activities with the family group.

Development Equivalents for Objectives (Expectations for younger or less mature students):

1. Has a growing appreciation of the importance of the family in society.
2. Is growing in understanding of each member's responsibility in family plans and projects, and in a desire to consider the wishes and needs of other members of the family.
3. Is eager to achieve some independence of the family and is beginning to find ways of doing so that gain family approval.
4. Is interested in understanding why younger children sometimes seem to be "pests."
5. Enjoys participating with other family members in some type of creative activities in the home.

SPEECH-COMMUNICATION, HIGH SCHOOL AND COLLEGE, COGNITIVE DOMAIN*

1. Given a 15 minute quiz you are to diagram a communication model of your choice and subsequently list each component of the model and describe in writing its function within the model. A minimum level of acceptance will be considered the inclusion and correct description (as

*The following objectives were developed by Donald J. Cegala and Elizabeth J. Lance for "Fundamentals of Speech Communication" at Purdue University. These objectives are reprinted by permission of the authors.

given in class) of at least the most basic and fundamental components of a communication model (as discussed in class).

2. Presented with a diagram of Johnson's communication model as discussed in class, in 15 minutes you are to define in writing *each stage* of the model and specify its function by describing *its relationship to at least two other stages* in the model. The criteria to be used in evaluating your responses are: (1) the correct (as given by Johnson) definition of each stage of the model; (2) the correct (as given in class) specification and description of each stage's relationship to *at least two other* stages in the model.

3. Given a 15 minute quiz, you are to diagram and label a structural differential as presented in class and in the assigned readings. You must then describe in writing how the relationships among the components of the diagram relate to Korzybski's general semantics. The criteria to be used in evaluating your responses are:

(1) The correct (as presented in class and assigned readings) diagraming and labeling of the structural differential.

(2) The correct (as presented in class) description of the relationships among the components of the structural differential and Korzybski's general semantics.

(3) "Correct" will be considered as the inclusion of all *main ideas* as presented in class and assigned readings.

4. Given the task of constructing an outline for a speech you must: identify *all* the main ideas of your speech as discussed in class and in the assigned readings; identify and describe *at least two forms of support* for each main idea; identify *at least two interest devices* for each main point; and employ the appropriate form for an outline including an *introduction, conclusion* and *sequence of organization* as discussed in class. You must specify *all* of the above underlined items to receive a passing grade on this assignment.

5. Given a quiz consisting of a printed text of a speech approximately 3 typed pages in length, in 30 minutes you are to:

(1) Identify in writing at least 75% of all the forms of support (as discussed in class) used in the speech.

(2) Evaluate the quality of each form of support identified using the criteria discussed in class.

(3) Write a paragraph of approximately 70 words in length in which you identify and evaluate the type of organization patterns employed

in the speech. You must identify at least two types of organizational patterns and evaluate them using the criteria discussed in class.

6. Given a time limit of 3 minutes you must identify orally and describe your own viewpoint on a controversial issue using at least 3 pieces of information from written sources. After your presentation you must answer specific questions posed by the audience about your viewpoint on the issue. Criteria for an acceptable level of performance are: (1) a speech limited to 3 minutes; (2) the use of 3 pieces of information from books, speeches, magazines, etc.; (3) clarity in developing *one* viewpoint and in answering questions from the audience.

HEALTH EDUCATION, ELEMENTARY AND SECONDARY SCHOOL, COGNITIVE AND AFFECTIVE DOMAINS

A comprehensive approach to specifying objectives for elementary and secondary health education has been employed by the School Health Education Study. They first have defined several concepts in health education and then specified general objectives for three domains – cognitive, affective, and psychomotor – for each concept. Next they have specified behavioral objectives for each step in a progressive sequence that leads to achievement of the general objectives. Their approach is indeed laudable and deserves serious consideration as a model for curriculum analysis and design. Permission was not granted to reproduce examples of these objectives, but copies of their book are available: *Health Education: A Conceptual Approach to Curriculum Design.* School Health Education Study, St. Paul, Minnesota: 3-M Education Press, 1968.

APPENDIX B

A System for Defining Achievement Descriptions for a Teacher Education Program

The material contained in this Appendix was prepared in the fall of 1968 in the College of Education, Southern Illinois University, as part of a continuing analysis and description of the Teacher Education Program. The objective of the segment of the program which is presented here was to compile a complete list of the instructional achievements in terms of student performance for all courses in the Teacher Education Program. Perhaps the two most significant features of this system are: (1) the concept of defining instructional achievements, rather than instructional objectives (although once the instructional achievements are produced, they become instructional objectives by changing the verb tense) for the purpose of describing and communicating about a course of instruction; and (2) the relatively detailed analysis and classification of student achievement according to the (a) type of performance, (b) form of performance, (c) product of performance, and (d) content of achievement.

Although when this program was begun, instructors were only asked to identify the achievement performance and success criteria for their achievement descriptions, it was intended that a complete classification system would be introduced later.

INTRODUCTION

In the spring of 1968 a program was initiated for the purpose of analyzing and describing the Teacher Education Program in the College of

Education at Southern Illinois University. Essentially, the program consists of a continuing, comprehensive analysis and description of (1) the characteristics of the instruction provided in all phases of the Teacher Education Program; (2) the characteristics of the students receiving this instruction; (3) what the students learn to do as a result of this instruction; and (4) what the students do in their initial years in the teaching profession.

The primary reason this program was initiated was to obtain a baseline description of the present Teacher Education Program so that promising new instructional techniques, curricular change, personnel redeployment programs, etc., could be experimentally tested and the effects could be observed in the baseline data. If, for example, a new method of instruction resulted in an improvement in the quality of our student products, it could be adopted; if, on the other hand, the previously employed method proved superior, it would be reinstated. Thus, the eventual goal is a coordinated program in which important aspects of our Teacher Education Program are continually analyzed and evaluated to produce the best teachers possible with available resources.

The purpose of this document is to request instructors in the Teacher Education Program to participate in this project by supplying data for one of the categories mentioned above: "What students learn in their courses." More specifically, what is being requested is for you to supply the following information each quarter for courses which you teach:

1. A description of the things which students learn in your courses (*i.e.*, knowledge, skills, abilities, and attitudes, which we refer to as "achievement descriptions" and will explain later).
2. A list containing the names and record numbers of the students who complete your courses with an indication of the achievement descriptions which each student mastered (called "Student Achievement Report").

Three example achievement descriptions and an example of a Student Achievement Report for students completing a course for which achievement descriptions have been stated are shown on the following pages to give you an idea of what we are talking about before proceeding.

Achievement Description Recording Form

Achievement Description Title: Test Construction Ad No. 5

Dept. Educational Psychology Course No. 469 Title Measurement

Quarter Winter Year 1987 Instructor Mr. Statistic

* *

1. *Achievement Performance* (What the student did):

Constructed two alternative test items for each of ten instructional objectives for a unit in the area in which he plans to teach.

2. *Success Criteria* (How the performance was judged for success):

The test items appeared to be valid measures of the objectives based on the specifications presented in Popham's* audio-visual instructional unit.

*Popham, "Evaluation," Vimcet Series (Self- Instruction Center)

3. Type of Performance	6. Content of Achievement (the "knowledge" learned)
____ Recognition	x Association
____ Reproduction	x Concept
x Application	____ Principle
	x Procedure
4. Form of Performance	
Observable behavior: reading and writing	____ Translation
Where Performed: in class	____ Reasoning
Time allotted: 50 minutes	____ Analysis
	____ Synthesis
5. Product of Performance	____ Evaluation
Twenty written test items	x Execution

Achievement Description Recording Form

Achievement Description Title: Human Development Ad No. 6

Dept. Educational Psychology Course No. 526 Title Human Development

Quarter Fall Year 1967 Instructor Dr. Piaget

* *

1. *Achievement Performance* (What the student did):

The student, upon being presented with descriptions of a variety of human behaviors often exhibited by a particular age group in a closed-book essay examination:

a. analyzed the situation and stated the factors according to human development principles which appeared to be casusing or contributing to the problem.
b. from the descriptions of predominant developmental characteristics (emotional, social, intellectual, and physical), hypothesized the major problem(s) for which there should be concern.
c. proposed in writing various alternatives based upon his knowledge of human development principles that a teacher and/or parent might utilize to lessen the concern of those acting to solve the problem(s).

2. *Success Criteria* (How the performance was judged for success):

a. The factors identified must be reasonable causes of the problems presented (textbook* used as authority.).
b. The major problems hypothesized must be potentially "Major problems" (textbook).
c. Alternative solutions must be appropriate to each situation and be "reasonable" solutions (teacher judgment).

*McCandless, Children: Behavior and Development, 1967.

3. Type of Performance	6. Content of Achievement (the "knowledge" learned)
____ Recognition	X Association
____ Reproduction	X Concept
X Application	X Principle
	X Procedure
4. Form of Performance	
Observable behavior: reading and writing	X Translation
Where Performed: in class	X Reasoning
Time allotted: 2 hours	X Analysis
	X Synthesis
5. Product of Performance	X Evaluation
Essay exam paper	X Execution

Achievement Description Recording Form

Achievement Description Title: Motivation in the Classroom Ad No. 14

Dept. Education Course No. 275 Title Instructional Technology

Quarter Fall Year 1984 Instructor Dr. Motivated

* *

1. *Achievement Performance* (What the student did):

Demonstrated knowledge of the following motivational concepts on a 50-item multiple-choice test: arousal, curiosity, anxiety, frustration, expectancy, incentives, punishment, drive, aspiration, restitution, Ripple Effect, positive reinforcement, negative reinforcement.

2. *Success Criteria* (How the performance was judged for success):

45 items were correctly answered, based on information in Chapter 5 in the textbook*.

*DeCecco, The Psychology of Learning and Instruction, 1968.

3. Type of Performance	6. Content of Achievement (the "knowledge" learned)
x Recognition	x Association
___ Reproduction	x Concept
___ Application	x Principle
	___ Procedure
4. Form of Performance	
Observable behavior: reading and marking	___ Translation
Where Performed: in class	___ Reasoning
Time allotted: 50 minutes	___ Analysis
	___ Synthesis
5. Product of Performance	___ Evaluation
Test paper	___ Execution

Prior to continuing the discussion of achievement descriptions, a short explanation of the other report which is to accompany the list of achievement descriptions seems appropriate here. The Student Achievement Report is essentially a list which contains the names and record numbers of the students in your courses with an indication of the achievement descriptions which each student mastered.

An example of a Student Achievement Report is shown on the next page. You can see on the example that some students (Numbers 2, 4, and 9) mastered all sixteen achievement descriptions while the other seven students mastered fifteen or fewer.

The numbers of the "Achievement Descriptions Mastered" on the Student Achievement Report should match the numbers on the list of achievement descriptions, so that it will be possible to determine which specific achievement descriptions were and were not mastered by each student.

Student Achievement Report
(Example)

Dept. Education Course No. 264 Title Teaching Methods

Quarter Fall Year 1969 Instructor: Dr. Method

	ID Number	Name	Achievement Descriptions Mastered															
			1	2	3	4	5	6	7	8	9	10	11	12	13	14	15	16
1	94548	Abercrombie, Mary J.	x	x	x	x		x	x			x	x	x	x		x	
2	B4590	Adams, Linda P.	x	x	x	x	x	x		x	x	x	x	x	x	x	x	x
3	32175	Brown, Mark L.	x	x		x	x	x	x		x	x	x	x		x		
4	C2895	Cabot, George G.	x	x	x	x	x	x	x	x	x	x	x	x	x	x	x	x
5	72670	Davidson, John M.	x	x		x	x		x			x	x	x		x		
6	61146	Hudson, Laura J.	x	x	x	x	x	x	x	x	x	x			x		x	x
7	91742	Jones, David L.	x	x	x		x		x		x			x	x	x		
8	D6677	Lindsey, Karen B.	x	x	x	x	x		x	x	x	x	x	x		x	x	x
9	32535	Miller, David B.	x	x	x	x	x	x	x	x	x	x	x	x	x	x	x	x
10	C4567	Smith, Jayne W.	x		x	x	x	x	x		x	x	x	x		x	x	
11																		
12																		
13																		
14																		
15																		
16																		
17																		
18																		
19																		
20																		

The achievement description is a discrete "either/or" type of measure. The student either did or did not master the specified achievement description according to the instructor's standards of mastery. This approach omits a great deal of information regarding degrees of mastery and lack of mastery, and the major reason for this is to simplify the task of stating achievement descriptions, measuring student mastery, and communicating the results.

It is probably obvious that what we have defined as course achievement descriptions are written statements which describe a particular performance which a student exhibits at some time during, or at the completion of, a course of instruction. Achievement descriptions are quite similar to the explicit, or behavioral, instructional objectives which have had a recent resurgence of popularity. The major difference between the two is that behavioral objectives specify what an instructor intends for students to achieve and achievement descriptions specify what the students actually do achieve. Thus, in writing achievement descriptions, it is not necessary to attempt to predict and specify in advance all of the things students should be able to do upon completing a course; only what students do learn to do in a course is recorded.

Once the achievement descriptions for a course are produced, it should require minimal time and effort in future quarters to check off each achievement description for each student as he demonstrates mastery during the course. The addition, elimination, and alteration of achievement descriptions should also not demand a great deal of time. On the other hand, it would be grossly misleading not to emphasize that the original specification of the achievement descriptions for a course is an arduous and time-consuming task.

SYSTEM FOR SPECIFYING ACHIEVEMENT DESCRIPTIONS

The system for specifying achievement descriptions is presented first and is followed by a set of guidelines for using the system. It is hoped that you will be able to write achievement descriptions for your courses as a result of reading this information. If you find the information inadequate for achieving this goal, personal assistance will be available.

The system for specifying achievement descriptions which is presented here was devised specifically for the Teacher Education Analysis Program and incorporates some of the elements of Bloom's *Taxonomy of Educational Objectives: Cognitive Domain* (1956), Robert Mager's (1962) three-part instructional objectives, and Robert Gagné's (1965c) classification of eight types of learning.

Since it is presumed that the majority of the instructional objectives of courses in the Teacher Education Program are in the cognitive domain, the predominant emphasis in these guidelines is on this domain. The affective and psychomotor domains are not entirely ignored, however, as suggestions for recording achievement descriptions in each domain are provided near the end of the guidelines. Presently, no attempt will be made to classify achievement descriptions beyond course and departmental designation. Eventually, a system organized by functional teaching tasks will be developed.

As mentioned previously, an achievement description is a written statement which describes something a student learned to do in a course. Probably the most important characteristic of an achievement description is that it talks about the performance of students. Thus, the knowledge or content, or subject matter, that a student learned in a course is defined by how he demonstrated that he had learned it. For example, if a student learned how to compute the arithmetic mean in a course, this knowledge or ability would be defined by his performance when he "computed a mean" or "identified the correct procedure for computing a mean." Similarly, if a student learned the team-teaching method of instruction, the achievement description would indicate that he "verbally described the team-teaching method" or that he correctly "identified a written description of team-teaching" or perhaps that he "actually carried out the procedures involved in team-teaching."

Achievement descriptions then specify what a student learned to do in a course, and there are six characteristics of achievement performance which are identified in an achievement description. These six are:

1. *Achievement Performance:* a one- or two-sentence description of the student's performance (what the student did when demonstrating his achievement).
2. *Success Criteria:* the specification of the criteria used to judge whether the student's achievement performance was successful (number correct on a test, qualities required of a term paper, etc.).

3. *Type of Performance:* whether the student's performance was predominantly a demonstration of recognition, reproduction, or application.
4. *Form of Performance:* brief descriptions of the publicly observable behavior employed in the performance (such as writing, speaking, etc.), where the performance occurred (in class, library, etc.), and the amount of time allotted for the performance (one hour, 3 weeks).
5. *Product of Performance:* what the student produced which the instructor examined to determine whether the performance was successful (test, 3- to 5-page paper).
6. *Content of Achievement:* the "knowledge" which the student learned and demonstrated in the achievement performance; specifically, which of four types of "knowledge" were employed in the student's performance (association, concept, principle, or procedure).

The process of specifying an achievement description consists of making decisions and recording information regarding these six characteristics. The form used for recording achievement descriptions is arranged to facilitate this decision-making and recording procedure.

Each of the six achievement description characteristics is defined and explained more fully on the following pages.

1. *Achievement Performance*

This is a brief description of what the student did in demonstrating achievement of one aspect of a course of instruction. Several examples of achievement performances are provided.

(What the student did)

a. Taught a single concept and evaluated whether or not it has been learned within a period of seven minutes. A critique of the presentation was made by the class members in terms of the learning activities selected to bring the referent to the students, amount of student involvement, whether or not the concept was learned, and the voice, poise, and mannerisms of the teacher. He summarized the suggestions made for improvement and stated those he would select for implementation and the steps he would take to implement them.
b. Wrote ten educational objectives which were behavioral according to Mager's criteria, at least three of which would be classified in

each of the following categories: affective, higher-than-lowest cognitive, and psychomotor.

c. Listened to a taped classroom situation involving a discipline problem and after analysis wrote a dialogue demonstrating alternative teacher behavior which is less of a personal affront and thus more behavior oriented, "supportive rather than rejectory," and "non-threatening" as identified by Amidon and Hunter.
d. Wrote examples of how the following principles could be applied to classroom management: positive and negative reinforcement; shaping; discrimination; generalization; punishment.
e. Developed a plan for a unit of instruction which took into account the individual differences of pupils.
f. Wrote a description of how Guthrie's contiguity theory of learning could be applied to classroom instruction.
g. Selected the most appropriate statistical test for a given set of data.

2. *Success Criteria*

This refers to the standards used for judging successful achievement performance. There are several ways to specify success criteria and the most appropriate one is usually determined by the kind of performance being judged. For example, with objective tests, an appropriate success criterion would be the number or percentage of total items which must be correct. Other examples are shown below.

(How the performance was judged for success)

a. It matched a particular model (for example, the performance was similar to that in the textbook or to that presented in class or to that shown in a film).
b. An acceptable number or percentage was correct.
c. The student's viewpoint was different from any of those discussed or covered in the reading.
d. He performed acceptably all of the functions of a discussion leader.
e. The application was appropriate for the given situation.
f. He operated the equipment and machines in the manner specified in the operator's manual.
g. The lesson plan employed the form presented in the textbook and appropriate procedures were applied in each step – according to the principles presented in class.

3. *Type of Performance*

This refers to which of the three types of performance was the predominant one employed when the student demonstrated mastery of the achievement description. The three types of performance are:

A. *Recognition:* This is when the student makes a response which indicates that he "knows" or "understands" something but he does not reproduce his "knowledge." Typically, this is when he makes a correct discrimination or identifies, or selects, correct information.

B. *Reproduction:* This refers to instances in which the student reproduces information (*e.g.*, verbal, figural) or a response sequence (*e.g.*, operating a calculator) which is similar both in form and content to that which he acquired in learning.

C. *Application:* This refers to performances in which the student applies some knowledge or information he has learned to complete a task which, in part or as a whole, has not been previously completed. This type of performance is commonly referred to as "transfer" and embodies a wide range of performance, from the application of knowledge of how to solve arithmetic problems to solving specific arithmetic problems, all the way to the application of a general strategy for producing a creative effort in the arts. The essential characteristics of this category of performance are that whatever was learned is performed on new information.

Most often, achievement descriptions will require a combination of all three types of performance; however, it is desirable to attempt to identify the most predominant type of response employed.

4. *Form of Performance*

Observable behavior: This characteristic refers to the publicly observable actions made by a student when he demonstrated achievement (*e.g.*, writing, speaking, marking, drawing, reading, operating, constructing).

Where performed: Where the performance occurred (in the classroom, outside the classroom, in the library, while observing a second-grade classroom, etc.).

Time allotted: The amount of time allotted to the student for performing the achievement (*e.g.*, in 50-minute class period, a two-week period, approximately one month, etc.).

5. *Product of Performance*

This refers to what the instructor looks at to determine whether a student has mastered an achievement description. Typically, this will be some kind of examination or assigned paper or a live performance in a classroom. Some examples are as follows:

Essay test
Short answer test
Multiple-choice test
Oral interview
Term paper
Three written lesson plans
3- to 5-page paper
Written curriculum plan
Project report
Research project prospectus
20-frame linear program
Oral statements made in class
Performance in audio-visual lab
Performance in first-grade classroom

6. *Content of Achievement*

This is the "knowledge" or content which the student learned and demonstrated in the achievement performance. Frequently, achievement performances employ more than one of the categories of content listed below and all categories employed should be identified on the achievement description form.

A. *Association:* name, fact, rule, description, definition, which refers to a specific object or event (*e.g.,* "mother," "12 inches is equal to one foot," "Wednesday," "Europe," a poem, an account of the Civil War).
B. *Concept:* a set of objects or events which have some characteristic in common but which differ from each other on other characteristics (*e.g.,* chair, round, courage, method of instruction, intelligence).
C. *Principle:* "If-then" statements usually concerning two or more concepts (*e.g.,* "if the temperature is raised, then the pressure goes up"; "if knowledge of results is supplied promptly, then the probability of the response is increased").

D. *Procedure:* a sequence of actions or events (*e.g.*, the scientific method, operating a drill press, how a bill goes through Congress, summarizing a chapter, evaluating a work of art, analyzing a poem, writing a term paper, designing an experiment). An important class of procedures are the six "application responses" defined below. When the type of performance, described previously, is "application," one or more of these procedures are often employed in the application.

1. *Translation:* the transfer of given information into a different form (*e.g.*, paraphrase, condense, summarize, expand).
2. *Reasoning:* deductive – inferring particulars from the general; inductive – inferring the general from the particulars, (*e.g.*, predicting trends.)
3. *Analysis:* breaking a whole into component parts (*e.g.*, identifying the parts of a flower, distinguishing facts from opinions).
4. *Synthesis:* composing something new from component parts (*e.g.*, writing an essay, formulating an hypothesis, devising a new game, producing examples of a concept).
5. *Evaluation:* judging an object or situation on the basis of certain criteria (*e.g.*, locating logical fallacies in arguments, judging a work of art, judging the quality of a textbook).
6. *Execution:* following steps in a sequential pattern, carrying out a plan of operation (*e.g.*, using a scientific method, designing a new course, solving mathematics problems – frequently this procedure incorporates the use of one or more of the other five procedures, such as in problem solving which typically employs analysis, synthesis, and evaluation).

This concludes the description of the system used in specifying achievement descriptions. Although the system may appear unduly complex on first encounter, it is hoped that its comprehensiveness will serve to simplify the task of specifying achievement descriptions once it is understood.

GUIDELINES FOR SPECIFYING ACHIEVEMENT DESCRIPTIONS

Possibly the most efficient way to learn the previously described system is to write down a one-sentence description of one of the things students learned to do in your course in the Achievement Performance section of the Achievement Description Recording Form. Next, specify how you measured the success of the performance. Then proceed to the other four points on the form. In making decisions regarding the appropriate classifications of the achievement performance, you will probably need to review the classification systems. It may also be necessary to restate some of the performance descriptions and success criteria originally specified after making decisions regarding the other components of the achievement description. Referring to the example achievement descriptions on pages 165, 166, 167, 168 and 169, which are for various areas in education, should also prove helpful.

If you already have explicit objectives specified for your course, it should be a relatively simple matter to translate them onto the Achievement Description Recording Form. If this is not the case and you find it somewhat difficult to begin to formulate some of the things students learn to do in your courses, you may find it valuable to look at, or just think about, the tests and other means used for evaluating student learning. For example, multiple-choice and true-false test items always require a "recognition" type of performance, and a "marking" form of performance. Of course, the information in the test must be examined to determine the content of performance. This concludes the specific suggestions for "how to do it." There is, however, some further information of a general nature which should further clarify the task of specifying achievement descriptions.

Criterion for acceptable achievement descriptions. Since the purpose of achievement descriptions is to communicate what students learn to do in your course, this is the criterion against which they should be judged. Probably the best test of an achievement description is whether other instructors in your field of specialty can independently produce a test or other evaluation procedures for evaluating a student's achievement performance which you agree is a valid measure of the achievement performance.

Amount of performance included in achievement descriptions. Achievement descriptions can be written for many different amounts of performance. They can be written with such specificity that one course would require 237 achievement descriptions; for example, the achievement performance statement for such a "micro-achievement" description might be: "The student wrote a definition of Thorndike's Law of Effect." At the other extreme might be achievement descriptions that include so much performance that three of four achievement descriptions might cover an entire course; for example, "The student completed short answer exams over the learning theories of Guthrie, Tolman, Thorndike, Skinner, Kohler, and Mowrer." Somewhere in the middle of this continuum seems desirable; for example, "The student specified, in writing, three major implications of the contiguity, reinforcement, and Gestalt theories of learning for classroom instruction."

Also, it is possible to write achievement descriptions for prerequisite steps which lead to terminal performances. For example, a student may first learn to write a definition of reinforcement and next learn to describe applications of reinforcement. Since being able to perform the latter usually implies the ability to perform the former, it seems most economical to specify only the latter.

Although it is difficult to make an estimate which fits all courses in our Teacher Education Program, it would seem that somewhere between ten and thirty achievement descriptions would be appropriate for most courses. The important thing is that all of the learning outcomes for your courses be included.

Time of achievement. Frequently, students learn things and are evaluated early in a course and are not re-evaluated over this subject matter during or upon completion of the course. Thus, it is possible that they may not be able to demonstrate the same level of mastery at the end of the course as they did earlier. Similarly, it is commonly found that a considerable amount of forgetting occurs soon after completion of a course. Thus, it was decided to only be concerned with the fact that a particular achievement was demonstrated sometime during or at the end of a course.

This approach should not, however, be taken as an indication that the retention of learned performances is considered irrelevant. On the contrary, whether something is retained for future use is really the only thing that counts. But since each course of instruction can only be concerned with the performances acquired in that course, the "course" achievement descriptions are restricted to achievements observed during the course. (Perhaps as a result of this analysis program, the need may be made apparent, and provisions developed, for systematic practice and review during students' programs to insure a high degree of retention and potential transfer after completing their education.)

Specifying affective and psychomotor achievements. Since it is presumed that the majority of the instructional objectives of courses in the Teacher Education Program are in the cognitive domain, the predominant emphasis in these guidelines is on this domain. The affective and psychomotor domains should certainly not be ignored, however, since in many cases it is feasible to observe attitudinal preferences by means of rating forms, *performance* statements may refer to students' "responses on a questionnaire. . .," or "ratings on an attitude scale. . . ." In addition, since attitudinal objectives are usually concerned with changing or maintaining attitudes during a particular time period, the information in *criteria* will typically say something about the amount of change in attitudes from the beginning to the end of a course. It should be noted that a quite worthy attitudinal objective for many students is for them to indicate at least the same level of preference toward something (like teaching or educational psychology) at the end of the course as they indicated at the beginning.

Due to the observable and measurable properties of psychomotor achievement, special instructions for their specification appears unnecessary.

Inclusion of performance measures. Whenever possible, copies of tests, assignments, and attitude inventories, should be appended to achievement descriptions. Such information can greatly facilitate communication regarding student achievement.

More Examples. On the pages which follow are several examples of achievement descriptions for various subject areas in education which you may wish to examine for further clarification or to refer to when you are writing achievement descriptions for your courses.

Achievement Description Recording Form

Achievement Description Title: Teacher Ethics Ad No. 7

Dept. Educ. Philosophy Course No. 298 Title Philosophy of Educ.

Quarter Spring Year 1967 Instructor Dr. Phil O'Soffer

* *

1. *Achievement Performance* (What the student did):

Described in writing at least eight situations which demonstrated four ethical and four unethical behaviors of teachers. A different ethical principle was illustrated in each situation.

2. *Success Criteria* (How the performance was judged for success):

Each situation was illustrative of one of the ethical principles stated in the NEA Code of Ethics.

3. Type of Performance	6. Content of Achievement (the "knowledge" learned)
____ Recognition	____ Association
____ Reproduction	____ Concept
x Application	x Principle
	____ Procedure
4. Form of Performance	
Observable behavior: writing	____ Translation
Where Performed: out of class	____ Reasoning
Time allotted: one week	____ Analysis
	____ Synthesis
5. Product of Performance	____ Evaluation
2-5 page paper	____ Execution

Achievement Description Recording Form

Achievement Description Title: Instructional Method Research Ad No. 3

Dept. Education Course No. 302 Title Methods of Instruction

Quarter Winter Year 1968 Instructor Dr. Empiric

* *

1. *Achievement Performance* (What the student did):

Conducted a thorough literature search and wrote a review of the major theories and experimental findings for one method of instruction (e.g., lecture, discussion, programed instruction) which is typically employed in the area in which the student plans to teach.

2. *Success Criteria* (How the performance was judged for success):

The review:

1. included the most important theories and studies for the chosen method.
2. correctly interpreted the literature.

3. Type of Performance	6. Content of Achievement (the "knowledge" learned)
____ Recognition	x Association
____ Reproduction	x Concept
x Application	x Principle
	x Procedure
4. Form of Performance	
Observable behavior: reading and writing	x Translation
Where Performed: library; personal study area	x Reasoning
Time allotted: 4 weeks	x Analysis
	x Synthesis
	x Evaluation
5. Product of Performance	x Execution
10-20 page paper	

Achievement Description Recording Form

Achievement Description Title: Projection Equipment Operation Ad No. 12

Dept. Instructional Technology Course No. 316 Title A-V Eqpt. and Mat'ls.

Quarter Summer Year 1966 Instructor Dr. Projector

* *

1. *Achievement Performance* (What the student did):

Operated 3 types of 16mm projectors, 2 types of 8mm projectors, 2 types of slide projectors, and 2 types of filmstrip projectors.

2. *Success Criteria* (How the performance was judged for success):

Projectors were correctly set up, loaded, operated (including sound and visual image adjustments), dismantled (including film rewinding), and returned to storage room. Each projector was set up and operating in less than 5 minutes.

3. Type of Performance	6. Content of Achievement (the "knowledge" learned)
____ Recognition	x Association
x Reproduction	____ Concept
____ Application	____ Principle
	x Procedure
4. Form of Performance	
Observable behavior: machine operation	____ Translation
Where Performed: A-V laboratory	____ Reasoning
Time allotted: three hours	____ Analysis
	____ Synthesis
5. Product of Performance	____ Evaluation
correctly set-up and operating machines	x Execution

Achievement Description Recording Form

Achievement Description Title: Teacher Role Preparation Ad No. 18

Dept. Secondary Education Course No. 372 Title Methods

Quarter Spring Year 1969 Instructor Mr. Teacher

* *

1. *Achievement Performance* (What the student did):

Indicated on a pre-post attitude rating scale that he maintained his perception of the role of the secondary teacher as a ''non-directive resource person,'' or that he changed to this position from the perception of the secondary teacher as an ''authoritarian teller.''

2. *Success Criteria* (How the performance was judged for success):

The student responded in one of the two locations next to the ''non-directive resource person'' role on a four-point rating scale at the end of the course.

3. Type of Performance	6. Content of Achievement (the "knowledge" learned)
_____ Recognition	_____ Association
_____ Reproduction	_____ Concept
_____ Application	_____ Principle
	_____ Procedure
4. Form of Performance	
Observable behavior: reading and marking	_____ Translation
Where Performed: in class	_____ Reasoning
Time allotted: 5 minutes	_____ Analysis
	_____ Synthesis
5. Product of Performance	_____ Evaluation
Rating scale	_____ Execution

APPENDIX C

Instrumentation of Bloom's and Krathwohl's Taxonomies for the Writing of Educational Objectives *

During the past six or eight years an increased amount of attention has been given to the statement of educational objectives in behavioral terms both to facilitate the evaluation of educational programs and to improve the validity of the measures and scales utilized in the evaluation process (Metfessel and Michael, 1967; Michael and Metfessel, 1966). Although set up as a programmed learning text, Mager's (1962) *Preparing Instructional Objectives* has been one of the most useful guides to teachers and specialists in curriculum who have sought help in stating the desired outcomes of instruction in behavioral language – in describing the kinds of specific and relatively terminal behaviors which the learner will be capable of exhibiting subsequent to his exposure to a program of instruction. Another useful source has been the volume edited by Lindvall (1964) who, in collaboration with Nardozza and Felton (Lindvall, Nardozza, and Felton, 1964) not only prepared his own chapter concerned with the importance of specific objectives in curricular development, but also enlisted the aid of several distinguished educators, e.g., Krathwohl (1964) and Tyler (1964) with specialized interests in evaluation. Such efforts have essentially involved a fusion of curriculum design with the evaluation process in that curricular planning is described in terms of behavioral

*Newton S. Metfessel, W. B. Michael, and D. A. Kirsner, "Instrumentation of Bloom's and Krathwohl's Taxonomies for the Writing of Educational Objectives," *Psychology in the Schools,* Vol. VI, No. 3 (July, 1969), pp. 227-231. This article is reprinted by permission, for which the authors express their thanks.

objectives that are necessary for the construction of valid tests and scales. The taxonomies provide the required model necessary to furnish meaningful evidence regarding the attainment of desired behavioral changes.

Although Krathwohl (1964) related the taxonomy of educational objectives in both the cognitive (Bloom, 1956) and the affective (Krathwohl, Bloom, and Masia, 1964) domains to curriculum building, he was able to present only a limited number of concrete illustrations, some of which Mager would probably challenge because of their relative lack of specificity. Admittedly, Krathwohl has made an important and helpful start in relating objectives to a meaningful and rather well-known conceptual framework. However, the writers believe that there exists a need for an instrumentation of the taxonomy of educational objectives within both the cognitive and affective domains – that is, a more clear-cut description of how the taxonomy can be implemented in the school setting. The approach utilized was the development of *behaviorally oriented* infinitives which, when combined with given objects, would form a basis for meaningful, cohesive, and operational statements.

PURPOSE

Thus the essential purpose of this paper was to show how specific behavioral objectives can be formulated within the hierarchy of the major levels and sublevels of the taxonomies of educational objectives as set forth by Bloom (1956) and Krathwohl (1964). Such a framework should furnish a helpful base around which behavioral statements of objectives can be formulated.

DEFINITION

An educational objective consists of a description of the behaviors of an individual (the learner or examinee) in relation to his processing information embodied in subject matter – that is, what the learner must be capable of doing with certain characteristics or properties of subject matter. The behavioral component, which may be described as a process involved at an appropriate level of the taxonomic classification, is usually expressed in the form of a noun "ability" or a verb of being "able" followed by an infinitive such as the "ability to do" or "able to do." The second component of the objective, which consists of the specific content often found in the formal learning experience (e.g., in the curricular or instructional unit), constitutes a direct object of the verb or infinitive form. The terms "subject matter" or "content" are used in a fairly broad sense, as their level of specificity is highly variable, depending upon the characteristics of the curricular unit.

INSTRUMENTATION

To facilitate the formulation of statements of specific behavioral objectives within the framework of Bloom's taxonomy, the writers have included a table made up of three columns. The first column contains the taxonomic classification identified by both code number and terminology employed in Bloom's (1956) taxonomy. The entries in the second column consist of appropriate infinitives which the teacher or curriculum worker may consult to achieve a precise or preferred wording of the behavior or activity desired. In the third column somewhat general terms relative to subject matter properties are stated. These direct objects, which may be expanded upon to furnish specificity at a desired level, may be permuted with one or more of the infinitive forms to yield the basic structure of an educational objective – activity (process) followed by content (subject matter property). At the discretion of the reader the words "ability" or "able" can be inserted in front of each of the infinitives.

TABLE I INSTRUMENTATION OF THE TAXONOMY OF EDUCATIONAL OBJECTIVES: COGNITIVE DOMAIN

Taxonomy Classification		KEY WORDS: Examples of Infinitives	KEY WORDS: Examples of Direct Objects
1.00	Knowledge		
1.10	Knowledge of Specifics		
1.11	Knowledge of Terminology	to define, to distinguish, to acquire, to identify, to recall, to recognize	vocabulary, terms, terminology, meaning(s), definitions, referents, elements
1.12	Knowledge of Specific Facts	to recall, to recognize, to acquire, to identify	facts, factual information, (sources), (names), (dates), (events), (persons), (places), (time periods), properties, examples, phenomena
1.20	Knowledge of Ways and Means of Dealing with Specifics		
1.21	Knowledge of Conventions	to recall, to identify, to recognize, to acquire	form(s), conventions, uses, usage, rules, ways, devices, symbols, representations, style(s), format(s)
1.22	Knowledge of Trends, Sequences	to recall, to recognize, to acquire, to identify	action(s), processes, movement(s), continuity, development(s), trend(s), sequence(s), causes, relationship(s), forces, influences

TABLE I (continued)

Taxonomy Classification		KEY WORDS Examples of Infinitives	Examples of Direct Objects
1.23	Knowledge of Classifications and Categories	to recall, to recognize, to acquire, to identify	area(s), type(s), feature(s), class(es), set(s), division(s), arrangement(s), classification(s), category/categories
1.24	Knowledge of Criteria	to recall, to recognize, to acquire, to identify	criteria, basics, elements
1.25	Knowledge of Methodology	to recall, to recognize, to acquire, to identify	methods, techniques, approaches, uses, procedures, treatments
1.30	Knowledge of the Universals and Abstractions in a Field		
1.31	Knowledge of Principles, Generalizations	to recall, to recognize, to acquire, to identify	principles(s), generalization(s), proposition(s), fundamentals, laws, principal elements, implication(s)
1.32	Knowledge of Theories and Structures	to recall, to recognize, to acquire, to identify	theories, bases, interrelations, structure(s), organization(s), formulation(s)
2.00	Comprehension		
2.10	Translation	to translate, to transform, to give in own words, to illustrate, to prepare, to read, to represent, to change, to rephrase, to restate	meaning(s), sample(s), definitions, abstractions, representations, words, phrases

TABLE I (continued)

Taxonomy Classification		KEY WORDS: Examples of Infinitives	KEY WORDS: Examples of Direct Objects
2.20	Interpretation	to interpret, to reorder, to rearrange, to differentiate, to distinguish, to make, to draw, to explain, to demonstrate	relevancies, relationships, essentials, aspects, new view(s), qualifications, conclusions, methods, theories, abstractions
2.30	Extrapolation	to estimate, to infer, to conclude, to predict, to differentiate, to determine, to extend, to interpolate, to extrapolate, to fill in, to draw	consequences, implications, conclusions, factors, ramifications, meanings, corollaries, effects, probabilities
3.00	Application	to apply, to generalize, to relate, to choose, to develop, to organize, to use, to employ, to transfer, to restructure, to classify	principles, laws, conclusions, effects, methods, theories, abstractions, situations, generalizations, processes, phenomena, procedures
4.00	Analysis		
4.10	Analysis of Elements	to distinguish, to detect, to identify, to classify, to discriminate, to recognize, to categorize, to deduce	elements, hypothesis/hypotheses, conclusions, assumptions, statements (of fact), statements (of intent), arguments, particulars

TABLE I (continued)

Taxonomy Classification		KEY WORDS: Examples of Infinitives	KEY WORDS: Examples of Direct Objects
4.20	Analysis of Relationships	to analyze, to contrast, to compare, to distinguish, to deduce	relationships, interrelations, relevance, relevancies, themes, evidence, fallacies, arguments, cause-effect(s), consistency/consistencies, parts, ideas, assumptions
4.30	Analysis of Organizational Principles	to analyze, to distinguish, to detect, to deduce	form(s), pattern(s), purpose(s), point(s) of view(s), techniques, bias(es), structure(s), theme(s), arrangement(s), organization(s)
5.00	Synthesis		
5.10	Production of a Unique Communication	to write, to tell, to relate, to produce, to constitute, to transmit, to originate, to modify, to document	structure(s), pattern(s), product(s), performance(s), design(s), work(s), communications, effort(s), specifics, composition(s)
5.20	Production of a Plan, or Proposed Set of Operations	to propose, to plan, to produce, to design, to modify, to specify	plan(s), objectives, specification(s), schematic(s), operations, way(s), solution(s), means
5.30	Derivation of a Set of Abstract Relations	to produce, to derive, to develop, to combine, to organize, to synthesize, to classify, to deduce, to develop, to formulate, to modify	phenomena, taxonomies, concept(s), scheme(s), theories, relationships, abstractions, generalizations, hypothesis/hypotheses, perceptions, ways, discoveries

TABLE I (continued)

Taxonomy Classification		KEY WORDS: Examples of Infinitives	KEY WORDS: Examples of Direct Objects
6.00	Evaluation		
6.10	Judgments in Terms of Internal Evidence	to judge, to argue, to validate, to assess, to decide	accuracy/accuracies, consistency/consistencies, fallacies, reliability, flaws, errors, precision, exactness
6.20	Judgments in Terms of External Criteria	to judge, to argue, to consider, to compare, to contrast, to standardize, to appraise	ends, means, efficiency, economy/economies, utility, alternatives, courses of action, standards, theories, generalizations

Although within a given major process level or sublevel of the taxonomy each infinitive cannot in all instances be meaningfully or idiomatically paired with every direct object listed, many useful permutations of infinitives and direct objects that furnish entirely readable statements are possible. Certainly use of these tables should lead to a substantial gain in the clarity and speed with which teachers and curriculum specialists, as well as those involved in construction of achievement tests, may state curricular objectives. The writers have found that these tables have been of considerable help to their students, as well as to personnel in public schools who are concerned with writing objectives prior to curriculum development, constructing test items, or to carrying out evaluation studies. Slight modifications can be made with the entries to meet the requirements of specific learning situations.

INSTRUMENTATION: AFFECTIVE DOMAIN

The instrumentation of the Affective Domain is the same as that of the Cognitive Domain, to wit, the selection of behaviorally oriented infinitives combined with selected direct objects. As in the case of the Cognitive Domain, these are to be conceptualized as examples for the stimulation of other infinitives and objects and, more important, meaningful objectives in a total framework.

TABLE II INSTRUMENTATION OF THE TAXONOMY OF EDUCATIONAL OBJECTIVES: AFFECTIVE DOMAIN

Taxonomy Classification		KEY WORDS Examples of Infinitives	Examples of Direct Objects
1.0	Receiving		
1.1	Awareness	to differentiate, to separate, to set apart, to share	sights, sounds, events, designs, arrangements
1.2	Willingness to Receive	to accumulate, to select, to combine, to accept	models, examples, shapes, sizes, meters, cadences
1.3	Controlled or Selected Attention	to select, to posturally respond to, to listen (for), to control	alternatives, answers, rhythms, nuances
2.0	Responding		
2.1	Acquiescence in Responding	to comply (with), to follow, to commend, to approve	directions, instructions, laws, policies, demonstrations
2.2	Willingness to Respond	to volunteer, to discuss, to practice, to play	instruments, games, dramatic works, charades, burlesques
2.3	Satisfaction in Response	to applaud, to acclaim, to spend leisure time in, to augment	speeches, plays, presentations, writings
3.0	Valuing		
3.1	Acceptance of a Value	to increase measured proficiency in, to increase numbers of, to relinquish, to specify	group membership(s), artistic productions(s), musical productions, personal friendships

TABLE II (continued)

Taxonomy Classification		KEY WORDS Examples of Infinitives	Examples of Direct Objects
3.2	Preference for a Value	to assist, to subsidize, to help, to support	artists, projects, viewpoints, arguments
3.3	Commitment	to deny, to protest, to debate, to argue	deceptions, irrelevancies, abdications, irrationalities
4.0	Organization		
4.1	Conceptualization of a Value	to discuss, to theorize (on), to abstract, to compare	parameters, codes, standards, goals
4.2	Organization of a Value System	to balance, to organize, to define, to formulate	systems, approaches, criteria, limits
5.0	Characterization by Value or Value Complex		
5.1	Generalized Set	to revise, to change, to complete, to require	plans, behavior, methods, effort(s)
5.2	Characterization	to be rated high by peers in, to be rated high by superiors in, to be rated high by subordinates in	humanitarianism, ethics, integrity, maturity
		and	
		to avoid, to manage, to resolve, to resist	extravagance(s), excesses, conflicts, exorbitancy/exorbitancies

REFERENCES

Bloom, B. S. (Ed.), Englehart, M. D., Furst, E. J., Hill, W. H. and Krathwohl, D. R. *A Taxonomy of Educational Objectives: Handbook I, the Cognitive Domain.* New York: Longmans, Green, Co., 1956.

Krathwohl, D. R. The Taxonomy of Educational Objectives – Its Use in Curriculum Building. In C. M. Lindvall (Ed.), *Defining Educational Objectives.* Pittsburgh: University of Pittsburgh Press, 1964. Pp. 19-36.

Krathwohl, D. R., Bloom, B. S., and Masia, B. *A Taxonomy of Educational Objectives: Handbook II, the Affective Domain.* New York: David MacKay Co., 1964.

Lindvall, C. M. (Ed.) *Defining Educational Objectives.* Pittsburgh: University of Pittsburgh Press, 1964.

Lindvall, C. M., Nardozza, S., and Felton, M. The Importance of Specific Objectives in Curriculum Development. In C. M. Lindvall (Ed.). *Defining Educational Objectives.* Pittsburgh: University of Pittsburgh Press, 1964. Pp. 10-18.

Mager, R. F. *Preparing Instructional Objectives.* Palo Alto, California: Fearon Publishers, 1962.

Metfessel, N. S. and Michael, W. B. A Paradigm Involving Multiple Criterion Measures for the Evaluation of the Effectiveness of School Programs. *Educational and Psychological Measurement,* 1967, 27 (Part II), 931-943.

Michael, W. B. and Metfessel, N. S. A Paradigm for Developing Valid Measurable Objectives in the Evaluation of Educational Programs in Colleges and Universities. *Educational and Psychological Measurement,* 1967, 27, 373-383.

Tyler, R. W. Some Persistent Questions on the Defining of Objectives. In C. M. Lindvall (Ed.), *Defining Educational Objectives.* Pittsburgh: University of Pittsburgh Press, 1964. Pp. 77-83.

APPENDIX D

Instructional Objectives Exchange

Never before in this country have we had so many educators committed to the idea that instruction should be evaluated primarily by the results it produces in learners. But even though many educators are aware of the merits of criterion-referenced instruction, few of them use operationally stated objectives in their instruction and evaluation efforts. Teachers, school district personnel, everyone involved in the day-to-day job of education are often too burdened by the demands of their jobs to embark on the difficult, time-consuming task of personally constructing stated objectives and related evaluation measures.

James Popham, who has been a champion of the behavioral objectives movement for the past five years, has observed that the widespread enthusiasm for behavioral objectives has not been matched by their widespread production and use. As a result, he has developed what appears to be a most promising solution. As a project of the Center for the Study of Evaluation at the University of California at Los Angeles, Dr. Popham has organized an Instructional Objectives Exchange to serve as a depository for objectives and measures; to provide a dissemination service; and to develop needed objectives and evaluation devices.

Educators committed to criterion-referenced instruction can now draw on the resources of this central clearinghouse, which will provide sets of instructional objectives and evaluation measures.

All objectives made available by the Objectives Exchange will be stated operationally, that is, in terms of measurable learner behaviors. All evaluation measures (not only test items but also diverse types of learner performance measures) will be based on these operationally stated objectives.

The primary service of the Objectives Exchange is to make available alternative objectives and measuring devices to assist school personnel in their instructional and evaluation activities.

We strongly encourage all people concerned with instruction to support the Exchange by *contributing* their operationally stated objectives and evaluation measures and by *withdrawing* objectives and items that are suitable for their particular instructional situation.

Direct all inquiries, documents, and correspondence to:

Instructional Objectives Exchange
Center for the Study of Evaluation
Graduate School of Education
University of California
Los Angeles, California 90024

W. James Popham is Director of the Instructional Objectives Exchange. Marvin C. Alkin is Director of the Center for the Study of Evaluation.

Index

Abilities and skills, 51
  definition, 51
Abstraction (*see* Conceptualization)
Acceptance of values, 61, 186
  example, 126
Accuracy of performance, 40 (*see also* Performance standards)
  example, 40-41
Achievement, 38
  content, 158-160, 165, 168, 173-76
  time of, 171
Achievement description, 157
  amount of performance included, 170
  characteristics, 164
  compared to instructional objectives, 163
  criterion for acceptability, 170
  definition, 164
  examples, 158-60, 173-76
  guidelines for specifying, 169
  recording form, 158-60, 173-76
  specifying, 163
Achievement performance, 158-60, 164-65, 173-76
Achievements:
  affective, 172
  psychomotor, 172
Acquiescence in responding 59, 186
Action terms, 78
Action words, 35
Affective behaviors, 136
Affective domain, 44, 55
  example, 125, 128, 132, 148, 152, 155
  instrumentation, 185
Alkin, Marvin C., 190
Amidon, E. J., 135
Ammerman, Harry L., 31, 42
Analysis, 53, 92, 169, 182
  of elements, 53, 182
  objectives, 93
  of organizational principles, 53, 183
  of relationships, 53, 183
Application, 53, 92-93, 167, 182
  objectives, 93
Applying a rule, 36
Arnstine, D. G., 119
Association, 168
Attending (*see* Receiving)
Attention:
  controlled, 58-59
  selected, 58-59
Attitude, 61
Attitudinal objectives, 101
Attitudinal questioning, 99
Attitudinal responses, 100

Awareness, 57, 186
of conditions, 125

Behavior, 32
Behavioral analysis, 31
definition, 32
Behavioral domains (*see* Cognitive, Affective, Psychomotor domains)
interrelationships, 46
Behavioral objectives:
and administrators, 107
application to specified educational levels, 102
controversial issues, 23
definition, 1
and environment of the school, 109
function, 1, 5
and parents, 109
relationship to participants in the educational process, 105
sample, 134
and school boards, 108
and students, 106
and teachers, 106
Behaviors, trivial learner, 116
Beliefs, 61
Bloom, B. S., 21, 31, 45, 47, 56, 92, 102, 116, 164, 177-79
Board of trustees, 108
Bobbitt, F., 105

Cardinal Principles of Secondary Education, The, Educational Policies Commission of the National Educational Association, 20
Carroll, J., 31
Cegala, Donald J., 153
Center for the Study of Evaluation, 189
Central Purposes of American Education, The, Educational Policies Commission of the National Education Association, 20
Certainty, 62
Characterization, 66, 187
by a value or value complex, 65, 187
Charters, W. W., 105
Chenzoff, A. P., 34
Children: Behavior and Development, B. R. McCandless, 159
Class orientation, 136
Classification of objectives, reasons for, 44
Cognitive domain, 44, 47, 137, 140, 143
instrumentation, 185
sample, 128, 132, 146, 153, 155
teacher education program, 164
Cognitive learning sequence, 135
College, 132, 137, 140, 143, 153
Commitment, 62-63, 187
Committee on Education, 108
Communication behaviors, non-verbal, 71
Communication objectives, for college, 146
Complexity of tasks and grade levels, 103
Components (*see* Planning objectives)
Comprehension, 52, 92-93, 181
Comprehension objectives, 93
Concepts, 131, 168
Conceptualization, 63-64
of a value, 63, 187
Constraints, 39, 40 (*see also* Performance standards)
Constructing Behavioral Objectives, Henry H. Walbesser, 35
Controlled action, 186
Conviction, 62
Coordination:
hand-ear, 70
hand-eye, 70
hand-eye-foot, 71
Criterion, 38

DeCecco, John P., 20, 31, 102, 140, 160
Decoding, 73
Demonstrating, 36
Describing, 35
Derivation of abstract relations, 54, 183
Developing Attitude Toward Learning, Robert Mager, 101
Discipline interaction, 135
Distinguishing, 35

Ebel, Robert L., 38
Economics, 137
Educational environment (*see* School environment)
Educational measurement, 38
Educational objective:
  definition, 178
  general, 20
  informational, 20
  innocuous, 120
  planning, 20
  precision, 122
  types, 20
Educational Objectives, W. James Popham, 116
Educational outcomes, 118
Educational Policies Commission, 20
Educational Psychology, 140
Edwards, A. J., 102
Elementary Statistics: Data Analysis for the Behavioral Sciences, Paul A. Games and George R. Klare, 143
Elementary school, 151
Elementary School Objectives, Nolan C. Kearney, 151
Encoding, 73
English language arts, 148
Esthetic development, 151
Evaluation, 3, 13, 55, 73, 93, 169, 184
  criterion-referenced, 25-26
  factors, important, 14
  functions, 26
  norm-referenced, 25-26
  objectives, 94
  standards, 38
  summary, 17
Execution, 169
Extrapolation, 52, 182

Facial expression, 72
Failure, causes, 13
Faith, 62
Feedback loop, 13-14, 17
Felton, M., 177
Folley, J. D. Jr., 34
French, Will, 21, 152
Fundamental skills, development of, 130

Gagné, Robert, 2, 4, 30-33, 103, 164
Games, Paul A., 143
General Model of Instruction, 1, 2
  flow diagram, 2, 3
  functions, 2, 17
  premise, 2, 17
  summary, 17
  test, 18
Generalized set, 65, 187
Gentry, A. N., 128
Gestures, 72-73
Glaser, Robert, 2, 20, 31, 103
Graduated sequence, 9
Guidance, 8
Guilford, J. P., 4

Health Education, 155
Health Education: A Conceptual Approach to Curriculum Design, School Health Education Study, 155
High school, 148, 152-53
Horrocks, J. E., 38
Human development, 133
Hunter, E., 135

Identifying, 35
Individual differences, 9
Individualized instruction, 24, 136
Informational objectives, 21 (*see also* Educational objectives)
  affective domain, 98
  characteristic, 77
  cognitive domain, 92
  content, 30
  differences from planning objectives, 28
  programed practice in writing and identifying, 79
  psychomotor domain, 101
  purpose, 30
  value, 22

Instruction:
related to democracy, 119
success, 14
Instructional achievements, 156
Instructional objectives, 3, 6-7, 13
analysis, 4
changes, 14
classification, 3
preparing, 3
selection, 3
specification, 4
summary, 17
Instructional procedures, 3, 7, 13
changes, 14
design, 7
summary, 17
Instrumentation:
affective domain, 185
cognitive domain, 185
Interpersonal Speech Communication, John Keltner, 146
Interpretation, 36, 52, 182

Jackson, P. W., 119
Judgments:
in terms of external criteria, 55, 184
in terms of internal evidence, 55, 184
Junior high school, 128

Kearney, Nolan C., 21, 151
Keltner, John, 146
Kibler, R. J., 22, 106
Kirsner, D. A., 47, 92, 98, 177
Klare, George R., 143
Knowledge, 47, 57, 92-93, 180
of classifications and categories, 50, 181
of conventions, 49, 180
of criteria, 50, 181
of dealing with specifics, 180
of methodology, 50, 181
objectives, 93
of principles and generalizations, 51, 181
of results, 9
of specifics, 48-49, 180
of terminology, 48, 180
of theories and structures, 51, 181
of trends and sequences, 49, 180
of universals and abstractions, 50, 181
Knudson, Rozanne, 21, 148
Komisar, P. B., 119
Krathwohl, D. R., 3, 21, 45, 47, 56, 177

Lance, Elizabeth J., 153
Lange, P., 31
Lazarus, Arnold, 21, 148
Learning activities, spontaneous, 117
Lindvall, C. M., 21, 177
Loyalty, 62

McCandless, B. R., 102, 159
McCann, J., 9
McClellan, J. E., 119
McDonald, F. J., 102
McHenry, Vere A., 132
McKenzie, William R., 104
McNeil, J. D., 22
Mager Robert, 4, 9, 20, 22, 39, 101, 116, 164, 177-78
Masia, B. B., 47, 56, 178
Mastery level, 39 (*see also* Performance standards)
Measurement, 118
difficulties, 120
Melching, W. H., 31, 42
Message invention, 73
Metfessel, N. S., 47, 92, 98, 177
Michael, W. B., 47, 92, 98, 177
Miles, D. T., 22, 106
Miller, R. B., 31, 34
Model of terminal performance (mastery), 8
Motivation, 8
Motor skills (*see* Psychomotor domain)
Movements:
bodily, 68-69, 72
finely coordinated, 69

hand-finger, 70
hand-foot-eye-ear, 71
lower limbs, 68
upper limbs, 68
M-STEP Monograph, Utah State Board of Education, 132
Munro, T., 120

Naming, 35
Nardozza, S., 177
Noble, C. E., 67
Non-verbal communication behaviors, 71
Nunnally, J. C., 38

Objectives:
classification, 44
for commitment, 147
for decision-making, 147
for non-verbal communication, 146
for problem-solving, 147
Observable behavior, 167
and grade levels, 104
Ordering, 35
Organization, 63, 73, 187
of a value system, 63-64, 187

Paden, D. W., 137
Payne, D. A., 38
Perceptual-motor skills (*see* Psychomotor domain)
Performance, 32-33
product, 158-60, 165, 168, 173-76
type, 158-60, 165, 167, 173-76
Performance form, 158-60, 165, 167
Performance measures, 172
Performance standard, 38-40
Pettigrew, L. E., 22, 106
Planning a Continuous Science Program for all Junior High School Youth, A. N. Gentry, 128
Planning objectives, 21, (*see also* Educational objectives)
components, 33-34, 36-38
content, 30
differences from informational objectives, 28
difficulties in specifying, 41-42
purpose, 30
value, 22
what to include, 37
Popham, W. James, 2, 20, 24, 115-16, 158, 189-90
Practice, 9
Practice exercises, 5, 10, 16
Pre-assessment, 3, 6-7, 13, 132
changes, 14
resulting courses of action, 7
summary, 17
Preference, value, 62, 127, 187
Pre-learning preparation, 8
Preparing Instructional Objectives, Robert Mager, 4, 177
Pre-specifying objectives, 24
Principle, 168
Product, 33 (*see also* Performance)
Production:
of a plan, 54, 183
of a unique communication, 54, 73
Psychology in the Schools, Vol. VI, No. 3, 177
Psychology of Learning and Instruction: Educational Psychology, The, John P. DeCecco, 140, 160
Psychomotor domain, 44, 66
classification, 68
sample, 146, 151

Reasoning, 169
Receiving, 56, 73, 186
Recognition, 167
Reinforcing student behavior, 134
Reproduction, 167
Responding, 58, 73, 186
active, 8
adequacy of, 38
Results, unanticipated, 122-23

Satisfaction in response, 60, 63, 186
Scannell, D. P., 102
Schaefer, H. H., 31
School:
elementary, 155

environment, 109
and behavioral objectives, 109
secondary, 125, 155
School board, 108
School Health Education Study, 155
Science, 125, 128
Scientific values, development of, 28
Scriven, M., 31
Selected action (*see* Controlled action)
Selected Objectives for the English Language Arts Grades 7-12, Arnold Lazarus and Rozanne Knudson, 148
Selecting Appropriate Educational Objectives, W. James Popham, 116
Social studies, 152
Sound-gesture coordination, 74
Sound production, 73
Sound projection, 74
Sound-word formation, 74
Specification of planning objectives, reasons, 30-31
Specificity continuum, 20
Speech behaviors, 73
Speech communication, 153
Stating a rule, 36
Statistics, elementary, 143
Stolurow, L. M., 31
Student achievement report, 156-57, 161-62
Student teaching, 136
Success criteria, 158-60, 164, 166, 173-76
Summary Report NSSA-NSTA Workshops on Behavioral Objectives, 155
Synthesis, 54, 73, 92, 94, 169, 183

Taber, J. I., 31
Task analysis, 31
Task description, 31
Taxonomy, rationale for, 45
Taxonomy of behaviors, drawback, 46
Taxonomy of educational objectives:
affective domain, 45, 56, 186
cognitive domain, 45, 47, 180
Taxonomy of Educational Objectives – The Classification of Educational Goals, Handbook I: Cognitive Domain, B. S. Bloom, et al., 47, 92, 164
Taxonomy of Educational Objectives – The Classification of Educational Goals, Handbook II: Affective Domain, D. R. Krathwohl, B. S. Bloom, and B. B. Masia, 47, 56
Teacher:
accountability for change, 121
expectations of, 119
role perception, 136
suggestions to, 41
Teacher education, 132
Teacher Education Analysis Program, 164
Teacher Education Program, 156-57
Teaching a concept, 134
Teaching loads, 122
Teaching methods, 133
Teaching performance, 9
Terminology, 131
Test:
construction and analysis, 135
preparation, 13
Theory generation, 131
Tiemann, P. W., 137
Translation, 52, 169, 181
Transmission, 73
Tyler, R. W., 31, 177

Unanticipated results, 122-23

Valuing, 61, 63, 186

Walbesser, Henry H., 35
Waples, D., 105
Where performed, 167
Willingness to attend, 58
Willingness to receive, 57, 186
Willingness to respond, 59-60, 186